LEGACY
Playbook

Kimberly
God's Favor & Blessings

JIMSUNDBERG.COM

LEGACY
Playbook

50 DAYS OF ENCOURAGEMENT TO PASS ON WHAT MATTERS MOST

A DEVOTIONAL

JIM SUNDBERG

3X ALL-STAR, 1985 WORLD SERIES CHAMPION,
6X GOLD GLOVE AWARD WINNER, TEXAS RANGERS HALL OF FAME

SUNDBERG LEADERSHIP TEAM | ARLINGTON, TEXAS

LEGACY PLAYBOOK

50 Days of Encouragement to Pass On What Matters Most

© 2020 Jim Sundberg.

All rights reserved. No part of this publication may be reproduced, distributed, or transmitted in any form or by any means, including photocopying, recording, or other electronic or mechanical methods, without the prior written permission of the publisher, except in the case of brief quotations embodied in critical reviews and certain other noncommercial uses permitted by copyright law. For permission requests, please contact the author.

ISBN (Print Edition): 978-0-9993652-1-2

ISBN (Kindle Edition): 978-0-9993652-2-9

Library of Congress Control Number (LCCN): 2020910158

Printed in the United States of America

Published by Sundberg Leadership Team | Arlington, Texas

Edited and prepared for publication by Wendy K. Walters | wendykwalters.com

Scripture Copyright Information:

> Scripture quotations marked ESV has been taken from The ESV® Bible (The Holy Bible, English Standard Version®). ESV® Text Edition: 2016. Copyright © 2001 by Crossway, a publishing ministry of Good News Publishers. The ESV® text has been reproduced in cooperation with and by permission of Good News Publishers. All rights reserved.

> Scripture quotations marked MSG are taken from THE MESSAGE, copyright © 1993, 2002, 2018 by Eugene H. Peterson. Used by permission of NavPress. All rights reserved. Represented by Tyndale House Publishers, Inc.

> Scripture quotations marked NIV has been taken from THE HOLY BIBLE, NEW INTERNATIONAL VERSION®, NIV® Copyright © 1973, 1978, 1984, 2011 by Biblica, Inc.® Used by permission. All rights reserved worldwide.

> Scripture quotations marked NLT are taken from the Holy Bible, New Living Translation, copyright © 1996, 2004, 2015 by Tyndale House Foundation. Used by permission of Tyndale House Publishers, Inc., Carol Stream, Illinois 60188. All rights reserved.

> Scripture quotations marked TPT are from The Passion Translation®. Copyright © 2017, 2018 by Passion & Fire Ministries, Inc. Used by permission. All rights reserved. ThePassionTranslation.com.

To contact the author:

JIMSUNDBERG.COM

Dedication

To my amazing wife, Janet—for your love, faithfulness, dedication, and support for nearly 50 years of marriage. You have been the love of my life since first meeting you when you were just 15.

To our children, Aaron, Audra, and Briana—you are walking out your faith in Christ with your sent-from-God mates, Cari, Chuck, and Stefon. Thank you for giving us ten wonderful grandchildren.

To my dad—I know you meant to be a good father and did the best you knew how. Your imperfections led me to chase after and wrestle with the one true, perfect Father, and His love for me knows no bounds.

Acknowledgement

I wish to express my gratitude to Wendy Walters—my comrade in arms on this project. Thank you for your vision and brilliance in editing my work.

LEGACY PLAYBOOK

Contents

INTRODUCTION	1
CHAPTER ONE—LOVE SOARS EAST	**3**
DAY 1—PASSION	5
DAY 2—MY DAD MY HERO	9
DAY 3—IDENTITY SPEAKS VOLUMES	13
DAY 4—KEEP YOUR ELBOW UP	18
CHAPTER TWO—ACTS OF TRUTH	**25**
DAY 5—TRUTH OR CONSEQUENCES	27
DAY 6—IRON SHARPENS IRON	31
DAY 7—FACT, OPINION, TRUTH	35
DAY 8—SPIN, EVADE, DEFLECT	40
DAY 9—KEEP SHOWING UP	44
CHAPTER THREE—BRILLIANT ECHO OF PURPOSE	**51**
DAY 10—HE'S GOT A PLAN	53
DAY 11—DISCOVERING UNIQUENESS	58
DAY 12—HOLD, HOLD, HOLD	62
DAY 13—IT'S ALL ABOUT THE TRAINING	66
DAY 14—THE LONG GAME	71
CHAPTER FOUR—TROUBLE IDENTIFIED	**79**
DAY 15—TROUBLE STRIKES	81
DAY 16—NO MISTAKES	86
DAY 17—SKILLED OPPONENT	89
DAY 18—A TIME FOR COURAGE	93
DAY 19—ISOLATION'S INVITATION	98
DAY 20—JUST DO IT	105
CHAPTER FIVE—TASTE OF THIRST	**109**
DAY 21—PRIORITIES	111
DAY 22—MY WAY	115
DAY 23—CHASING	119
DAY 24—QUEST FOR THE BEST	123
DAY 25—AIN'T NO SATISFACTION	128
DAY 26—PERSPECTIVE GAP	133

CHAPTER SIX—LOSS 139
- DAY 27—LOSS OF OUR BABY — 141
- DAY 28—KEEP SHOWING UP — 147
- DAY 29—LOSS OF LEGACY — 153
- DAY 30—ESCAPE TO FREEDOM — 156

CHAPTER SEVEN—GAME-CHANGING LENS 163
- DAY 31—A MORE LASTING APPROACH — 165
- DAY 32—GAME-CHANGING LENS — 169
- DAY 33—SAVED BY GRACE — 172
- DAY 34—SEEING GOD THROUGH THE WOUNDS — 176

CHAPTER EIGHT—A NEW PERSPECTIVE 181
- DAY 35—EYES TO SEE — 183
- DAY 36—FAVOR — 186
- DAY 37—THE UNCERTAINTY OF PERFORMANCE — 189
- DAY 38—HEALING EMOTIONS — 193

CHAPTER NINE—OBSTACLES TO OPPORTUNITIES 203
- DAY 39—BELIEF SYSTEMS — 205
- DAY 40—GOD IS AT WORK — 209
- DAY 41—WINDOWS — 212
- DAY 42—WRESTLE AND WAIT — 217
- DAY 43—UNDYING COMMITMENT — 220

CHAPTER TEN—MASTERFUL MENTOR 225
- DAY 44—LISTEN WELL — 227
- DAY 45—THE GIFT — 232

CHAPTER ELEVEN—ADVANCING PRESENCE 237
- DAY 46—RHYTHM OF TRAINING — 239
- DAY 47—SOMETHING WONDERFUL — 243
- DAY 48—THE DISCIPLINE OF PRACTICE — 249
- DAY 49—TAKING RISKS — 254
- DAY 50—I GOT THIS! — 260
- JIM'S PERSONAL MISSION STATEMENT — 267

PHOTO GALLERY 269

Introduction

A little over a year ago, I began to pen an allegory about a young man named Chosen living in the Land of Innocence. Along the way, he encounters many characters such as Love and Hope, who are pivotal to helping him meet the Legacy Giver and find his way into the Land of Legacy.

As he sojourns on a quest to define what matters most, he meets the Legacy Taker and his terrible Castle Guards. He experiences a taste of thirst, encounters loss, and must cross the River of Choices. Bit by bit, Chosen comes to know and understand who he was created to be and the legacy for which he was born.

As I wrote, I let my imagination run wild and often found myself mirrored in Chosen. Before long, I was writing my personal stories in between the allegory pages. These stories contain my own beginnings in the Land of Innocence and the long journey toward the Land of Legacy. In January of 2020, just before the global pandemic shut the world down, I sat down with a friend in a coffee shop, and she encouraged me to share these personal vignettes as a devotional. This book is the result of that prompting.

I have grouped my daily stories into chapter themes that will someday reflect the chapters of the allegory I hope to complete and publish. I share memories of my childhood and plenty of behind-the-scenes action during my MLB career. I am transparent about my battle with depression and my unhealthy drive for performance. Many of the stories are lighthearted and humorous, while others reveal deeply personal memories that have helped me heal emotionally and grow my character. This book is a tribute to God's amazing grace in my life!

I hope that as you work through this 50-Day Devotional, you will be challenged to reflect on your own life, sort through priorities, see yourself in a new light, and answer God's invitation to grow closer to Him.

Each day offers a short story, a promise from Scripture, a song, a few questions for mindful reflection, then a prompt to journal a prayer and write down what you hear the Father saying back to you. At the conclusion of each chapter, there is an invitation to reflect on the chapter's theme, and through that lens, determine what matters most to you.

Writing has been a pleasure. Reviewing these stories has helped me, and I hope it will help you too. So, as you set out on this 50-day quest with me, I pray you will learn that you too have been chosen.

Chapter One

LOVE SOARS EAST

"The Lord Himself goes before you and will be with you; He will never leave you nor forsake you. Do not be afraid; do not be discouraged."

—DEUTERONOMY 31:8

LEGACY PLAYBOOK

Day 1
PASSION

My Land of Innocence was located across the street from a ballpark. By age five, baseball was a passion—my first love. The ballpark became my second home. In the summer, there was seldom a time when I wasn't the first kid in the park in the morning and the last one to leave at night!

It was frustrating to be unable to hit home runs, so we brainstormed about what to do. Together, my buddies and I created smaller fields inside the main field. That way, we could hit "home runs" … at least until we were old enough to be able to hit real ones with the park's actual dimensions! This was pure joy and impossible to measure how much fun we were having. I did not yet know it, but this feeling of delight was passion's voice building a foundation in my heart for future accomplishments! This act of discovery—adventure and creativity unleashed toward a goal—would be a game-changer.

Each night when the lights turned off, we were met with disappointment, but this was buffered by the amazing freedom we had found in playing all day. There was always the hope of the next morning when sunlight presented us with a gift, like something left behind from Santa at Christmas. Only the prize wasn't under a tree; it was under a canopy of light. Each day the sun pushed away the shadows and gave us back our treasured playing field.

From the moment day broke, and light rushed into my window, excitement began. The treasure hunt was on as I raced to the park to investigate possible findings.

Our quest was to discover if any player or fan from the previous night's game had left a gem behind. Maybe a penny or dime had been carelessly dropped from the pocket of a spectator below the bleachers. Any coins found on the premises became our chance to score our favorite bubble gum chew just like the big leaguers (or so we thought back then)!

We couldn't afford baseballs, so our only hope was to obtain a misplaced or forgotten ball. We searched hard to find one left behind by some disenchanted player whose performance made him uncaring of the precious leather pearl with stitches. We scoured every inch of that park, hoping to find one of those white nuggets stuck in some dark corner or stashed in one of the cinder blocks stabilizing the wooden benches in a dugout.

There was a thrill in the pursuit of a white stained ball that was new every morning. Do it again tomorrow … and the next day … and the next day … whatever it takes. We showed up every day and pressed on for the find—constant discipline in pursuit of a treasure.

We are created to chase after something. Most of my life was spent chasing after baseball. The problem with chasing comes only when we pursue the wrong things. Baseball was an amazing chase, but it has never compared to pursuing after the greatest treasure of all: a personal relationship with God—the Legacy Giver!

We are created to chase after something!

Day 1 Meditation

PROMISE

> I have not stopped giving thanks for you, remembering you in my prayers. I keep asking that the God of our Lord Jesus Christ, the glorious Father, may give you the Spirit of wisdom and revelation, so that you may know Him better. I pray that the eyes of your heart may be enlightened in order that you may know the hope to which He has called you, the riches of his glorious inheritance in His holy people, and His incomparably great power for us who believe.
>
> EPHESIANS 1:16-19a, NIV

MUSIC

Listen to *I Can Only Imagine* by Mercy Me.

REFLECTION

- What treasure have you been chasing?

  _____

  _____

- Currently, where is your main passion? Does God have a place in that passion?

  _____

  _____

- What do you feel you are being led to do?

_____

_____

JOURNAL A PRAYER

_____

_____

_____

_____

_____

_____

_____

WHAT IS THE FATHER SAYING TO YOU?

_____

_____

_____

_____

Day 2
MY DAD MY HERO

My dad was my hero, as most kids want their dad to be. I desired an intimate connection with him, desperately wanted his notice, and sought his affirmation. He worked hard at two jobs just to provide for necessities. He never took time off. He epitomized the Postal Service Creed: "Neither snow nor rain nor gloom of night stays these couriers from the swift completion of their appointed rounds." A hard worker and loyal employee, when he finally retired from the U.S.P.S. after thirty-three years, he had an incredible fifteen months of sick leave built up.

While still young and living in my own Land of Innocence, my dad was good at playing amateur baseball in a summer league. While playing on a team, he generally hit third or fourth in the lineup, making him the best hitter on the team. He was a great defensive third baseman with a strong arm. I loved watching him play baseball. Dad was a cool dude with lots of energy … I wanted to be just like him!

He was good at fixing and creating things too. Neither dad nor I enjoyed chasing down balls, so he developed a system to eliminate this during batting practice. He drilled a hole through the ball and attached a string with a knot. This brilliant invention allowed us to increase our hitting time. I adored my dad and cherished this closeness and his enthusiasm for what I thought at the time was for me.

We would sometimes drive to Chicago to watch the Cubs play in Wrigley Field. Since we lived about 180 miles from our destination, dad would wake me up before the sun twinkled its first ray of light. I was always eager to rise, unable to sleep the night before a trip in anticipation of knowing the entire next day would be spent with my dad and baseball.

There were no interstates to travel, only beautiful two-lane roads with green cornfields boasting their bounty on each side, their neat rows revealing the richest coal-black soil in America. The fences bordering them seemed to move with us as we sped by, occasional fields of sprouting green beans popped up, only standing about a quarter of the height of corn. We would leave early, watch an afternoon game, and get back late

Baseball is one of the last pro sports a family can afford to enjoy together. Generations pass down their love for the sport, their loyalty to a team—legacy moments that tie families together down through history.

We made sure to arrive in time for batting practice. "Practice makes perfect," dad drilled. We never missed batting practice.

"Jim," dad would say never taking his eyes off the players on the field, "if you want to be good at anything, you need to practice. " My young mind seized on this truth, and thus practice became securely embedded into my DNA.

I loved it all—the ushers, the warm sun on my shoulders, watching the players … but there was one more reason for getting there in time for batting practice; some of the players batted balls into the seats down the left-field line where we always hung out. Score! More balls for practice with my buddies was golden!

It was uncanny the way we captured balls—and not just pre-game. It was as if the future was calling back to the present. God provided me with something we couldn't afford so I could do something I was called to do—address an interested audience with a message of encouragement. This field was the place of my childhood dreams … little did I know that twenty-five years later, I would stand to perform in that same arena.

These exhilarating days would gradually come to an end. My dad carried me off to bed as the dream world transitioned from reality back to fancy.

Day 2 Meditation

PROMISE

> See what great love the Father has lavished on us, that we should be called children of God! And that is what we are! The reason the world does not know us is that it did not know Him.
>
> 1 JOHN 3:1, NIV

MUSIC

Listen to ***How He Loves*** by Jeremy Riddle.

REFLECTION

- How was your relationship with your dad?

  _____

  _____

- Chances are your relationship with your earthly dad didn't accurately represent the love of God. Meditating on the Word of God is our opportunity to know His love for us. Ponder what it would look like to commit to experiencing this love! What might that look like to you?

  _____

  _____

  _____

JOURNAL A PRAYER

WHAT IS THE FATHER SAYING TO YOU?

Day 3
IDENTITY SPEAKS VOLUMES

Names are important. Have you ever noticed how, when you get someone's name wrong, they generally correct you right away? Calling a person by name communicates their value.

Years ago, I attended a Dale Carnegie class because of my inability to remember names, probably because at that time, I didn't see it as a way to express love to someone. In reality, there wasn't much care on my part to remember a person's name. They taught us to create mind pictures with names—an invaluable skill—and by the end of class, I had won the competition by remembering seventy-eight of eighty possible names of forty people.

There is nothing like being a Cubbie! I don't have to tell you how popular the Cubs are worldwide, wearing a Cubs uniform while playing in Dodger Stadium was a dream come true. I grew up a big Cubs fan. "Cubs, Cubs, Cubs, Cubs, …" I can't say it enough; the name rolls off the tongue repeatedly without harm to most ears except Cardinal fans. Who can dislike a teddy bear disguised as a Cub?

Anyway, toward the end of my career, while playing with the Cubs, while wearing that precious Cub uniform inside Dodger Stadium, the discovery of the importance of names became clearer.

In 1987 I was on the downside of my career, and I found my role on the team was to sit on the bench more often than desired. As a backup catcher does before game-time, I headed to the bullpen to warm up pitchers once the game started.

I moved out of the dugout onto the field, and fans began to say, "Sandberg, Sandberg, give me your autograph!"

Irritated, I pointed to the back of my jersey and, initially with a smile, said, "It's Sundberg ... Sundberg!"

In my entire ten-minute walk, this went on repeatedly. I dutifully stopped to sign autographs, but by the time I arrived at my destination, my patience had worn thin. I put my pen away, which is the most polite way to say, "I'm through with all this disrespect, I've played the game too long to deserve this!"

Usually, this confusion with the last name wasn't a problem, but Ryne Sandberg was a teammate, and we both had dark hair and bore some resemblance. (I wish he hadn't been so much better looking! ... Put the mask back on, Jim!)

The atmosphere in the bullpen that day was different. It was hard to read, and I couldn't put my finger on it. My 16-year old son Aaron had joined me for one of many family trips over the years. Could this be an issue? I thought to myself. But the thoughts of teammates being disturbed with his presence quietly vanished by their kind interactions with him.

Something, though I could not tell what, was suspiciously hanging in the air. I normally catch on quickly, but on this day, it took me three innings before I figured it out. I was sitting there watching the game, and it hit me like a wild pitch thrown into my ribs! Could it be? I thought ... NO! NO!

I got up to go to the restroom, attempting to fight off the panic. I closed the door behind me and made sure I was alone, then quickly, I turned to look in the mirror, grabbing and turning the back of my jersey to see the name. Stretching to pull my top to be visible in the mirror,

I read the back: SANDBERG. I was so humiliated. I stood there for a moment frustrated, furious … and then the funny hit me, and I burst into laughter!

Those who know me know I like a good joke. I thought to myself, Hold the line, SANDBERG, don't give in and don't let the others in the bullpen know that you know. I thought about how I would play this cool for the rest of the game. Maybe you can use this for your benefit, I thought.

I gathered myself together, then calmly walked out the door with my head slightly down, slightly glancing up with my eyes. All my teammates turned around, looking for a reaction. I didn't give it to them. For the next two innings, I played along without so much as an idea for payback coming to mind.

Just take it, SANDBERG! I told myself, It was a great joke … you probably deserved it. A few innings later, I finally acknowledged the prank, and the entire bullpen broke out in mass laughter.

I turned to my son Aaron, who, knowing precisely what I was thinking, said, "Dad, they threatened me if I told you."

"It's okay, son," I said, lightly punching his shoulder. He was aware of my playfulness as well, and deep down, Aaron probably felt some satisfaction and payback.

Rick Sutcliff had intentionally switched out jerseys in my locker, exposing just the "NDBERG" part of the name. I had a flippant way of throwing on the jersey top, so I had not noticed the switch. Innings later, I was finally called in to play the game, but not before a quick trip to my locker for an exchange.

Names are significant… to be known for who you are … especially in front of forty thousand fans!

Day 3 Meditation

PROMISE

> Lord, you know everything there is to know about me.
> You perceive every movement of my heart and soul,
> and you understand my every thought
> before it even enters my mind.
> You are so intimately aware of me, Lord.
> You read my heart like an open book and you know all the
> words I'm about to speak before I even start a sentence!
> You know every step I will take before my journey even begins.
> You've gone into my future to prepare the way, and in kindness
> you follow behind me to spare me from the harm of my past.
> With your hand of love upon my life,
> you impart a blessing to me.
> This is just too wonderful, deep, and incomprehensible!
> Your understanding of me brings me wonder and strength.
>
> PSALM 139: 1-6, TPT

MUSIC

Listen to ***What a Beautiful Name*** by Hillsong Worship.

REFLECTION

- God's awareness of us speaks volumes into our hearts. Do you believe that He is intimately aware of who you are?

_____

- Why do you feel this way?

  _____

  _____

- What action do you feel led to take to become more intimate with God?

  _____

  _____

JOURNAL A PRAYER

_____

_____

_____

_____

_____

_____

WHAT IS THE FATHER SAYING TO YOU?

_____

_____

_____

_____

Day 4
KEEP YOUR ELBOW UP

When I was ten years old, there was an incident that began to bring me out of my Land of Innocence. Looking back, it was the first time I recall that my dads' love was conditional on my performance. This event caused me to begin questioning my core value as a person, a state of mind that would end up haunting me for years and last well into my adult life.

During my youth, I was beyond my years as a baseball player. The league ages ranged from 9 to 12 years old; it wasn't like today where you play the same ages or maybe play up one year.

In this one life-changing game as a ten-year-old, I hit three home runs and struck out once. Not bad, huh? All I remember is that it was the best moment of my life. Even as I think back now, the memories are vivid with excitement elevating my heart to a new level.

I could tell that people observing the game, from either the field or the bleachers, were impressed. It's just the way an athlete picks up on his environment, and this sensitivity was happening early to me. There was a buzz. No one had seen this before in Galesburg, Illinois. "Who is this kid?" they wondered, but was dad awestruck as well?

After the game, I raced over to dad, "What-did-ya think?" I panted, joy all over my face!

"Jim," he answered, "The time you struck out, you dropped your elbow," my joy evaporated …" Next time keep your elbow up," dad finished his critique.

I was crestfallen. A fundamental shift occurred in my mind. My ten-year-old brain could not process that statement emotionally, but my ten-year-old heart heard, "You are falling short of perfection, Jim. If you want me to love you, then be perfect." My ten-year-old mind heard, "You're not good enough. You don't have what it takes."

Quietly though, dad was training me to be a Major League Baseball player as most around our neighborhood knew. Dad was attempting to capture lost dreams from his early years through my performance. All this attention, focus, and pressure on me were setting up a foundation of emotional anxiety and fear, a life of dealing with a depressed heart on and off for over four-five years. A life spent trying to win over love, approval, and acceptance of others through performance from the wrong places; the false tentacles of hope that drive a person in the ground compromising both physical and emotional health.

Glancing back, this was when I began to see a shift in dad's demeanor, becoming more on edge. His discipline began to be more emotional and angry. From this game forward, I would try harder and harder to win his approval. I would try to earn his love. This would haunt me for years!

A cycle began, and anxiety began to build in me. If I didn't have a perfect performance, I would get really down on myself … I did not like myself if I was not perfect. I didn't believe others would love me if I was not perfect.

These messages—these lies—locked me up emotionally and thwarted my ability to fully receive God's love and grace. I will never fully understand this understand until I go to be with Him. It affected my ability to love myself, and therefore, the ability to love others.

Besides my love for playing baseball and getting out to play in the summertime, it was also a cover for the sadness in my heart from a father that could terrify anyone in the family, including mom. I had no idea then how to put words to the sadness, fear, and anxiety that hovered the home like a dense dark cloud with the possibility of a pop-up storm breaking out at any moment with his presence.

This time in my life was when I started to run, carrying my mom's sadness and absorbing my dad's fear and anxiety. I couldn't get away from its emotional negativity. His behaviors would later cause a life of being in and out of depression or sad episodes.

Today, I realize that sometimes my episodes of sadness are created by realistic perceptions and the natural emotions surrounding them. At other times, however, my prolonged seasons of sadness have been distorted in some way and caused depression. These episodes were most intense during my MLB career. Thankfully, these have been fewer and farther between post-career. Only now am I beginning to put the pieces all together.

I wish I could tell you that I never fight depression anymore, but this is not the case. I still have times when I struggle, and I am so grateful for a loving wife and supportive family and friends who walk beside me when I am in the valley of shadows. Each time, though, I come out of an episode with a little more understanding of myself and who God wanted to be for me in those seasons.

I didn't believe others would love me if I was not perfect.

Day 4 Meditation

READ

Read the story of the Prodigal Son in Luke 15:11-32.

PROMISE

> "Let's prepare a great feast and celebrate. For this beloved son of mine was once dead, but now he's alive again. Once he was lost, but now he is found!" And everyone celebrated with overflowing joy.
>
> LUKE 15:23-24, TPT

MUSIC

Listen to **Good Good Father** by Chris Tomlin.

REFLECTION

- Have you ever failed at something or lost your way in this world? How did this make you feel?

_____

_____

_____

_____

- It's great to have forgiving arms waiting when you need them most. Perfection is not the goal in this life; we are working out the kinks. What was the last time you needed forgiving, unconditional love waiting for your return?

JOURNAL A PRAYER

WHAT IS THE FATHER SAYING TO YOU?

LOVE SOARS EAST

WHAT MATTERS MOST

Our priorities—the things which matter most—profoundly inform our thoughts and actions throughout each day. Our values serve to motivate us as well as guide us and provide direction. It is important to clearly define these guideposts. You don't discover them, you choose them.

In this chapter, the stories I shared were rooted in my identity—who I was and what I believed about who I was created to be. I often did not feel like I was enough, so I compared myself to an impossible ideal version of myself with whom I could never measure up. It took me many years to understand and embrace my God-given identity. Once I did, everything changed.

With this in mind, I encourage you to jot down what matters most to you concerning your identity.

_____

_____

_____

_____

_____

_____

_____

_____

_____

In a futile attempt to erase our past, we deprive the community of our healing gift. If we conceal our wounds out of fear and shame, our inner darkness can neither be illuminated nor become a light for others.

BRENNAN MANNING

Chapter Two

ACTS OF TRUTH

"For if you embrace the truth,
it will release more freedom into your lives."
—JOHN 8:32 TPT

LEGACY PLAYBOOK

Day 5
TRUTH OR CONSEQUENCES

When I was very young, at the beginning stages of acquiring a memory, my dad exercised an act of love that would shape my value for honesty and pursuing truth—not a bad legacy to leave your kids. There would be times when dad did stuff that was not wise, as all of us dads and moms will do, but on this particular day, my dad's love in action would impact my family and me for generations to come.

There was a corner grocery store close to the first house I ever remember. I love those ole' corner neighborhood grocery stores, like the convenience stores of today, but with more personable people. The owner lived next door and knew everyone in the neighborhood. He was like everyone's best friend and part of the family.

My dad took me with him to the store to pick up whatever it was my mom had sent him to buy. Being too young to grasp the give and take of commerce yet, apparently, I pocketed some candy during the trip without telling anyone. As we were walking the short distance back to our house, I was playing with my sister Linda, and I pulled the candy out to share some with her. Heck, dad brought things home from the store all the time … I wasn't trying to hide anything. I knew dad went to the store and came back with stuff for us. I guess I was aware of him visiting with the nice man behind the counter, but I had no concept that money was exchanged for the things we took home. I had no clue I had done anything wrong.

"Where did you get that?" dad asked sternly, his voice slightly raised. "Where did you get that candy?"

"At the store," I answered, no guile in me, but the tone in my dad's voice made my stomach do a little flip.

This was my first time to know what marching looked like, felt like … its pace, its purpose, and its intensity. Dad marched me straight back to the nice man's store.

"Tell him, son," dad said.

I looked down at the floor, uncomfortable; I had not meant to do anything wrong.

"I stole the candy," I almost whispered, "… and I'm sorry."

Dad counted out the coins and paid for the candy. He laid his hand on my shoulder as he led me out the door. I could feel the weight of it but was comforted by it just the same.

Tell the truth. Always tell the truth. Message received.

I did not yet know the meaning of the word integrity, but this act of love by my dad laid the foundation of it for me that day. I came to value truth—to always tell the truth, to confront what was not right, to take responsibility, and to realize there were consequences for my actions. It was easy to tell the truth that day but has not always been so easy as an adult.

Love tells the truth.

No legacy is so rich as honesty.
—WILLIAM SHAKESPEARE

Day 5 Meditation

PROMISE

> But those who love the truth will come out into the Light and welcome its exposure, for the Light will reveal that their fruitful works were produced by God.
>
> JOHN 3:21, TPT

MUSIC

Listen to ***O Come to the Altar*** by Elevation Worship.

REFLECTION

- Have you messed up big time? Have you committed a sin you believe so big it is unforgivable? Nothing is so big it can't be forgiven by the Father. Is there something you need to confess to restore fellowship with God? Do this now.

_____

_____

_____

_____

_____

_____

JOURNAL A PRAYER

_____

_____

_____

_____

_____

_____

_____

WHAT IS THE FATHER SAYING TO YOU?

_____

_____

_____

_____

_____

_____

_____

Day 6
IRON SHARPENS IRON

I made it to the Major Leagues on my defensive ability, and it took several years before my offensive skills matched the level of my defensive ones. After winning six American League Gold Gloves (it should have been nine, in my humble opinion), some saw my career as only a defensive specialist.

Though I had won six Gold Gloves in a row, things got interesting when I started to catch for knuckleballer, Charlie Hough. First of all, one doesn't catch a knuckleball—you wrestle it to the ground, step on it, and throw it back. The thrown ball dances and darts around like you are fighting the air, trying to trap a mosquito.

Several times, the ball hit my body without me ever even getting a glove on it. There was one time in Baltimore, during an early April snowstorm, that the wind was literally blowing snow in my eyes, and a knuckleball hit me, "Smack!" in the mask. My glove was somewhat close, but I never touched that ball. Man, I hated catching a knuckleball (even though Charlie said I was one of the best).

Hitting a baseball flying towards you at ninety-five miles an hour is one of the toughest skills in sports. Players who fail 70% of the time are All-Stars in baseball. NFL quarterbacks have to complete 50% of their throws. NBA players need to make 50% of their shots. Needless to say, hitting is tough, and so it took me almost three and a half years to beginning hitting in the Major Leagues.

A teammate helped me learn how to inside-out a ball and hit it to right field during practice for about a year before it actually started happening in a game. Finally, what was happening in practice began to translate into actual games starting around July 1, 1977.

Teammate John Ellis, who was a backup catcher, pulled me to the side one day to give me some needed advice, "Jim," he said, "if you don't start to hit, the manager is going to give me your job."

This sent shock waves through me. Being a celebrity, not many people (other than my family) often took the risk to confront me. It was uncomfortable. But John was a leader, and confronting me was the most effective means of getting me to address my issue and resolve it. He spoke the truth to me at the right time. My feelings didn't matter. My future did.

Seek not greatness, but seek truth and you will find both.
—HORACE MANN

ACTS OF TRUTH

Day 6 Meditation

PROMISE

> As iron sharpens iron, so one person sharpens another.
> PROVERBS 27:17, NIV
>
> People lose their way without wise leadership,
> but a nation succeeds and stands in victory when
> it has many good counselors to guide it.
> PROVERBS 11:14, TPT

MUSIC

Listen to ***Clear the Stage*** by Jimmy Needham.

REFLECTION

- Are you a person who is open to feedback, or are do you have it all figured out? The Bible talks about the wisdom of many counselors. In what areas would it be wise for you to seek the counsel of another?

_____

_____

_____

_____

- Write down who you will allow to speak into your life in each of these areas.?

_____

_____

JOURNAL A PRAYER

_____

_____

_____

_____

_____

_____

_____

WHAT IS THE FATHER SAYING TO YOU?

_____

_____

_____

_____

Day 7
FACT, OPINION, TRUTH

Wade Boggs was a 5-time batting champ, a 12-time All-Star, and an 8-time Silver Slugger winner, and was inducted into the Baseball Hall of Fame in 2005. These are facts—there is no denying the numbers. Documented facts are great to use.

It was my opinion, though, and with a high degree of certainty, that I knew the best way to get Wade Boggs out. It just so happened that my opinion was shared by two respected colleagues, Carlton Fisk, a Hall of Famer, and Bob Boone. Both were great catchers of the 70s and 80s, but our strategy was still just our opinion.

Fisk, Boone, and I became friends on a Nike All-Pro Club trip. While we played against each other, our times to share secrets came on this annual trip. We all looked forward to it every year the week after Thanksgiving.

Over ten years with this club (until my retirement), Nike took us to some fantastic destinations with our wives: Caribbean Island trips, Luxury Cruise Lines, Dude Ranch Adventures with every imaginable activity, Hawaiian Islands trips, etc. It was a good gig—we received a little money, got all the baseball cleats we needed, and there were even apparel offerings for the entire family at a time when having Nike clothing was expensive!

In the late 70s, Nike was moving toward the cleat market, so they started this club with about five of us. When I left the group, it had swelled to thirty, a bunch of future Hall of Famers and second-tier guys.

Hall of Fame players are in the top 1% of all players who wear an MLB uniform. I've been told I slot into the top 2%, therefore a second-tier player, and very happy to have arrived there. I certainly never expected to attain that status when I was growing up.

Early on, we tried out their cleat models during competition to give them feedback to refine their shoes until it met Nike's standards of excellence. Then, they took them to market. On this particular trip, Wade Boggs was along.

Fisk, Boone, and I knew that if Boggs, being a left-handed hitter, were allowed to hit a fastball to the left side of the field, he would hit around an average of .400. If we selected slower pitches, making him pull the ball to the right side of the field, he would hit close to .320 average, nothing really to get excited over, but 80 points better is good.

Wade Boggs and Tony Gwen were the two best hitters in baseball during the 80s and 90s—Wade in the American League and Tony in the National League. Their actual batting average stats would make this right even if others thought differently. This assessment is based on the interpretation of other essential elements such as players who, when the team needs a hit and run scored, may do it better and more consistently than the two players just mentioned. The idea of who the best hitters are then becomes an opinion based on interpretation—and there are good reasons for backing this notion.

Let me make a case for facts regarding Wade and Tony: Boggs played 18 years, hitting a .328 average with 3010 hits. On the other hand, Gwynn played 20 years with 3141 hits with a lifetime .338 average. This is data based on fact. But neither of their stats necessarily make them the best hitters in crucial situations. Their stats just mean they have the best averages (which are, indeed, very impressive). This is not to diminish either of the two hitter's accomplishments. Both have over twice as many hits as I mustered during my sixteen years!

If the best hitter argument was based not on averages, but instead on run production when teams needed a hit to score a run, then the answer to who is the best hitter may be different. After all, runs rule! So, if this is the lens looked through, then my best hitter analysis shifts to George Brett. In my estimation, he is the best hitter I ever played with or against. He hit better in these situations than anyone—and many others would agree with my opinion. George Brett is also a Hall of Famer, collecting 3,154 hits while hitting a .305 average over 21 years.

Whatever hit was needed at the moment, George was the best. First, get the runner over from second base to third base with a ground ball to the right side of the infield with no outs. Then, sac-fly with the runner at third base with less than two outs. Base hit to score a run with two outs and start an inning off with an extra-base hit to get himself into a scoring position with no outs. Lastly, get that game-important home run. Runs win games; a hit does not always drive in a score.

Facts and statistics are useful when making a statement. Opinions generally have some varying shades (or interpretations) of these facts and statistics (as applied to individual situations). However accurate either may be (or however great one's ability may be to persuade) facts, statistics, and opinions still do not fit the model for truth. Truth comes from God. Truth trumps facts, statistics, and opinions. Facts change. Statistics can be skewed. Opinions are unreliable. Truth remains.

Day 7 Meditation

PROMISE

> Jesus explained, "I am the Way, I am the Truth, and I am the Life. No one comes next to the Father except through union with Me. To know Me is to know My Father too."
>
> JOHN 14:6, TPT

MUSIC

Listen to **Holy Spirit** by Francesca Battistelli.

REFLECTION

- It's hard in today's world to know what is truth, what is opinion (even if well-founded) and what are lies. Truth is a person, and His name is Jesus. All truth comes from Him. Everything else folds in around this. Jesus is either a liar, a lunatic, or He is who He said He is. What do you believe about Jesus?

_____

_____

_____

_____

_____

_____

- What does the Word of God say about your circumstances—**the truth**—even in the face of facts which may seem to contradict God's promises?

JOURNAL A PRAYER

WHAT IS THE FATHER SAYING TO YOU (ABOUT YOU)?

Day 8
SPIN, EVADE, DEFLECT

My first year and a half of Major League baseball was spent playing for the fiery manager, Billy Martin. I know what you are thinking right now if you know baseball, "Bless your heart, Jim." (If one lives in Texas, you can say anything about anyone as long as you follow it up with, "… bless his heart!")

There were some great moments with Billy as he turned the 1974 Texas Rangers around. Initially, he was very good to me and often complimentary. The following year, however, would not be so inviting, and in some ways, would help facilitate his departure.

Since Billy was my first MLB manager, I had a certain level of respect for him. It was prudent to listen to what he said. It's easy to listen to a guy who is successful, but even more important to listen to one's manager. I kept telling people that his pistol range from underneath the bleachers just outside his office as you walked from the clubhouse to the dugout had nothing to do with his persona of intimidation!

Before my sixteen-year career would conclude, there would be fifteen more managers—four of them in one year, and two of the sixteen managers I would have twice. Do the math. That is eighteen manager changes in sixteen years! That will make your head spin.

In those early years, I was trying to learn how to call a game, so Billy was more than happy to assist with advice. "Jim," he said, "when you get into a tough situation, just look over to me, and I'll give you a signal for what to throw."

"Great!" I responded, glad for the assistance … at least I thought it was great at the time.

Every time there was a tough situation, I would look over to Billy for that signal, but he was always getting a drink of water or talking to someone and wouldn't look at me. I would wait uncomfortably long, the pitcher peering in with the sign to hurry up, but the promised glance never came from Billy.

After what felt like minutes, I would just go ahead and make the call, my head still glancing toward the dugout for any possible last-second sign—even while I began sending the pitcher a signal for what to throw next.

As far as Billy was concerned, if the ball ever got hit, it was the wrong pitch—even if it was right in the mind of Hall of Fame pitcher Fergie Jenkins and myself. But with Billy, if the batter hit the ball, it was the wrong pitch. Billy would flip out every time!

Once back to the dugout, I would have to answer the barrage from an angry manager. "Billy," I would interject, "… I was looking to get your attention, watching for you to signal …"

"Doesn't matter!" Billy would interrupt with exasperation, "What were you thinking? You should never have called for that pitch!"

Spin, evade, deflect. Never taking responsibility is what spin masters do. Truth has no part in them; they will compromise any promise to escape accountability. Leaders disclose, take the heat, and accept consequences. They embrace truth.

"Man must cease attributing his problems to his environment, and learn again to exercise his will—his personal responsibility."

—ALBERT EINSTEIN

Day 8 Meditation

PROMISE

> So above all, constantly chase after the realm of God's kingdom and the righteousness that proceeds from Him. Then all these less important things will be given to you abundantly.
>
> MATTHEW 6:33, NIV

MUSIC

Listen to ***The King is Here*** by Kim Walker-Smith.

REFLECTION

- At some point, we all are confronted with the opportunity to compromise either in our work or in our relationship with others. In what parts of your life have you compromised?

  _____

  _____

  _____

  _____

- Let Jesus take the regret and shame from you. It isn't too late. No matter how far back this was, or what consequences have been the result, it is never too late to step into truth. Write down "I am forgiven, Jesus paid this debt for me."

  _____

  _____

JOURNAL A PRAYER

WHAT IS THE FATHER SAYING TO YOU?

Day 9
KEEP SHOWING UP

If there was something to fear, my dad could find it. If there was nothing to fear, dad could invent a reason. These would start with, "Well, what happens if …?" I grew up with so many of these scenarios that I got really good at inventing them myself.

Several years into my Major League Baseball career, I would get the question, "Was there something early in your career that made you think you might not make it?"

My response was not what you might think.

"Yes," I would answer, "my fear of flying."

Yeah, they were puzzled when they heard my answer too! But the fear of flying was the thing that almost kept me from succeeding. It was not any lack of ability, not a lack of mental makeup, not a lack of desire. There was no shortage of energy, and certainly no lack of practice! I was simply terrified to fly. I had no reason to fear flying, I had never flown, but I was afraid anyway.

I was told by my dad to be afraid of flying. And so I was.

No one in my family had ever flown, but yet somehow, it was something we each feared. "What happens if the plane goes down?" my dad would say.

"Death," we could all announce the dreaded word. Something too awful to risk. Something else to fear! "What happens if …"

Before the time my first flight was to take place, I had worked up a really good froth of emotions. It was really gut-wrenching stuff with a stomach ache and all, and I hadn't even gotten on the plane yet, let alone in the air, and I was in knots.

I was a freshman at Iowa on my way to Arizona for spring break games. I really don't remember boarding the plane, but I took an aisle seat for two reasons: 1) so I could escape in case of problems; and 2) so I didn't have to look out the window.

The flight to Phoenix was a mere two-hours, but emotionally it felt like it took days to arrive. I looked at my watch every five minutes without taking my hand off the arm divider. Every one of those minutes seemed like an hour. The "What happens if …?" messages were giving me emotional hits, one after another. "What happens if my seat breaks free from below, and I tumble to my death?" … I rechecked my watch, "What if I have to jump and have no parachute?" Seriously, what makes someone think like this?

Not one bad thing had happened to me, but I had traumatized myself with all the worst-case scenarios that could possibly ever play out. I gave into my fear completely.

Unaddressed fear will have its way with a crippling effect, I know. I know what it's like to be in this place, but better yet—I know the way out!

It took several years to overcome my fear of flying. I did, at last, get free from this anxiety. I kept showing up because playing baseball was what God made me to do and to play baseball meant I had to fly. I didn't give up, and God manifested His power in each one of those moments even though tangible feelings of safety would not come until much later.

There was no one moment where I had a giant breakthrough. But looking back, each time I got on or off a plane and confronted my fear to walk out my destiny, the moments stacked together. When enough of these victory moments stacked together, it began to feel good, then powerful, and finally, freeing.

Today, I love flying in the window seat, often sleeping with my face leaned against a window. I know the energy it took to be free from my fear. There is nothing like this freedom, and it was worth every ounce of sweat and emotional blood spilled to get there. It was an act of stamina that God gave me to keep showing up in my life. Flying scared in order to walk in my destiny brought me freedom and paved the way to pursue my purpose.

Keep flying even if it scares you. Keep showing up. Living in purpose is worth confronting your fears.

Day 9 Meditation

PROMISE

> Don't be pulled in different directions or worried about a thing. Be saturated in prayer throughout each day, offering your faith-filled requests before God with overflowing gratitude. Tell him every detail of your life, then God's wonderful peace that transcends human understanding will make the answers known to you through Jesus Christ.
>
> PHILIPPIANS 4:6-7, NIV

MUSIC

Listen to ***No Longer Slaves*** by Jonathan David Helser (Bethel Music).

REFLECTION

- What are you afraid of? Is there something so terrifying that it keeps you from doing what you know God wants you to do? Write this down.

_____

_____

_____

_____

- Now, find promises in scripture to help you confront these fears and stand in truth. Write these verses down.

_____

JOURNAL A PRAYER

WHAT IS THE FATHER SAYING TO YOU?

ACTS OF TRUTH

WHAT MATTERS MOST

The stories in this chapter revolve around truth. Our social media culture has made it increasingly difficult to discern the difference between facts and opinions, between living "your truth" and the truth of God's Word.

Those who speak God's truth into our lives are rare and highly valuable. Walking in integrity matters. With your focus on how you handle speaking the truth and how much you value truth being spoken to you, write down what matters most to you.

_____

_____

_____

_____

_____

_____

_____

_____

_____

_____

_____

_____

> *Rather, speaking the truth in love, we are to grow up in every way into Him who is the head, into Christ.*
>
> EPHESIANS 4:15, NIV

Chapter Three

BRILLIANT ECHO OF PURPOSE

You make known to me the path of life;
You will fill me with joy in Your presence,
with eternal pleasures at Your right hand.

—PSALM 16:11, NIV

LEGACY PLAYBOOK

Day 10
HE'S GOT A PLAN

Since I was five years old, I was basically programmed to be a baseball player. Fortunately, this was also a dream of mine, and although the passion in me was real, the "programmed" part led to fractures in my relationship with dad.

I had just graduated from high school and was anticipating being drafted in the Major League Baseball Amateur draft held annually during the first week of June. No amateur player could be drafted until they were at least eighteen years old, and my whole family was on high alert to hear any news.

One week passed. No call.

Two weeks passed. Still no call. There was no long-awaited ring of the phone, no voice promising a spot on a professional baseball team. It was excruciating.

Things have changed since then. Today, if a player were drafted between the fifth and fifteenth rounds, he would not only have heard from several top baseball college coaches in pursuit, he would also have had a call from several Major League teams. It is typical now for teams to chase a player for weeks or even months before the draft. By draft day, a player has probably been on the phone several times, so an amateur player and his family generally know if he has been drafted the same day of the event. Back in my day, that wasn't the case.

Three long weeks passed before I finally received word about my draft, and even then, it didn't come by the ring of a phone. We were subscribed to a sporting newspaper, and an article suggested I had been drafted in the fifth round by the Oakland A's out of California. Other information referenced the fifteenth round, so we were confuse—but who cared? I had been drafted!

It was now late into July, and another month passed since we first read that news, and still, no one from Oakland had reached out to us about the draft. My dad didn't know what to do. We didn't have a plan to move forward without a call. I had been "trained" to play pro baseball; college wasn't an option we had even considered.

Six weeks passed, and not only did I not have a call from a MLB team, I hadn't even received a single scholarship offer from a college. Then something miraculous happened. Based on a letter of recommendation from my second-grade school teacher (who had graduated from the University of Iowa), the head coach, Dick Shultz, and his assistant (future head coach) Duane Banks, came to a summer league game where I was playing against an Iowa City American Legion team. These coaches didn't even have to leave their home base of Iowa City to see me play, and I played my best game ever. As a result, after the game, they offered me a full scholarship. I accepted.

Three days before the start of my first semester, the Oakland A's finally called. Roughly ten weeks after the draft date, I received a reasonably good offer of $16K. To my surprise, my dad declined the offer, and due to league rules, it would take another three years before I would have another draft opportunity.

───── • • • ─────

Finally, in June '72, the Rangers drafted me in the fifth round. The scout took Janet and me to lunch and tore my game apart. "Jim," he said, "you can't hit, you can't catch, and everything you throw goes to center field … but I'll give you a chance to play pro baseball for $6K."

Later, I would realize his job as a scout was to deflate a player's ability with the intent to lower his expectations, and hopefully, accept less money to play. It was not a pleasant experience for me.

Six months later, while still a senior at Iowa, Major League Baseball held their winter draft (they no longer do this). In the fall leading up to the draft, I had been contacted by several MLB clubs, and this time around, I received a call the very next day. In my third draft, and as their second pick, the Texas Rangers drafted me. Upon hearing this news, I was distressed. How could this be? I thought, The Rangers don't even like me, let alone think I can make it to the big leagues? This stinks!

The scout lived in Chicago, and he wanted to come to Iowa City to talk. After my last experience with a Rangers' scout, I was not eager to listen. We got together anyway, and he gave us his spiel adding a little more money—and this time, without the negative talk, so we listened. Janet advised me to call, Sam Suplizio, a coach I had played for in Grand Junction, Colorado, one summer. He had significant ties to baseball and could provide some much-needed perspective. I heeded his advice and made a call to the team's director for the minor leagues, bypassing the scout. After a brief discussion, we agreed to terms, and I became the property of the Texas Rangers.

I can now look back and can see there were two essential components to my success. Timing and confirmation. These are necessary ingredients in the recipe of purpose.

The process is all part of God's perfect planning.

Day 10 Meditation

PROMISE

> "For I know the plans I have for you," declares the LORD, "plans to prosper you and not to harm you, plans to give you hope and a future. Then you will call on Me and come and pray to Me, and I will listen to you. You will seek Me and find Me when you seek Me with all your heart."
>
> JEREMIAH 29:11-13, NIV

MUSIC

Listen to *I Am* by Mark Schultz.

REFLECTION

- Maybe you are in transition right now. Maybe one door has closed for you, and another hasn't opened yet. When that happens, it is easy to feel alone, and you can become unsure of God's plan for you. You start to question your purpose. Listen: God cares about you. God has a plan for you. He is at work in your present circumstances—even if it does not seem that way. Think about what is happening in your life right now. Identify some of the "ingredients" in God's recipe for your purpose. What are they?

_____

_____

_____

BRILLIANT ECHO OF PURPOSE

JOURNAL A PRAYER

WHAT IS THE FATHER SAYING TO YOU?

Day 11
DISCOVERING UNIQUENESS

Even though the sentiment may be expressed by many, I actually hate to hear the words, "It's a job." This is not what I think God had in mind for us. After my first year in pro ball, I worked the winter in a hometown factory in Galesburg, Illinois, putting compressors in the back of Admiral refrigerators. My fingers got more calloused from my work while squatting on the assembly line than it ever did from squatting behind the plate.

In the first two weeks, I found the assembly line to be a place of discovery because I was learning a new skill. I'm a front-end development-minded person, so this worked well. However, once I learned the skill and the discovery part of knowing how best to perform it was over, the need for repetitive maintenance set in. Maintaining anything is not something about which I get excited.

I quickly began to wonder what in the world I was doing there. I thought, I don't know how much longer I can look up this assembly line day after day and do this? It was not work I enjoyed at all, and I found myself saying, "I can't wait until the next break."

The thought of doing this work for an extended period (beyond the two months of winter before spring baseball) pressed hard on my emotions. It offered nothing for my creative juices to flow. From that mindset, I could see this as only a job, frozen by a lack of options. I had to make a shift in my thinking so that this work could become a motivator for something else. I needed to make what I was doing connect to my purpose. I needed to make this about baseball.

So, I connected squatting on the line to squatting behind home plate. Even working on something I did not enjoy, I discovered important elements about myself. What I took away from the experience would benefit me for that which I was created. That connection to purpose allowed me to press on with a much better attitude.

Day 11 Meditation

PROMISE

You formed my innermost being, shaping my delicate inside and my intricate outside, and wove them all together in my mother's womb.

I thank you, God, for making me so mysteriously complex!

Everything you do is marvelously breathtaking.

It simply amazes me to think about it!

How thoroughly you know me, Lord!

You even formed every bone in my body when you created me in the secret place, carefully, skillfully shaping me from nothing to something.

You saw who you created me to be before I became me!

Before I'd ever seen the light of day, the number of days you planned for me were already recorded in your book.

PSALM 139:13-16, TPT

MUSIC

Listen to **_Where Were You_** by Ghost Ship.

REFLECTION

- Think about what it is you most like to do. It takes courage to pursue your dreams and discover who you really are. To do this requires you to connect with the Father in how He created you, who He made you to be. Where are you in this discovery? What were you born for?

_____

_____

_____

_____

_____

_____

_____

_____

JOURNAL A PRAYER

WHAT IS THE FATHER SAYING TO YOU?

Day 12
HOLD, HOLD, HOLD

In 1989, during the last six weeks of my final year on the field, my manager, Bobby Valentine, decided to sit me on the bench for the remainder of the season to develop younger catchers. Thankfully, he did let me play my last game. Tom Grieve, former teammate, friend, and general manager, made sure I caught Nolan Ryan on my last day with a very nice pre-game tribute to my career.

There were about three weeks left in the season, and I knew I was nearing the completion of my playing days. I found myself sitting on the bench pre-game, pondering the terrifying thought of what would come after the September finish. I had no plan for what was next. Throughout my entire career, I was often haunted by the thought that an injury could end my playing days unexpectedly. I often sat in the dugout, wondering what I would do next if that were ever the case. Now, it was a looming reality.

As I sat there, Bobby Valentine came to me and said, "Jim, HSE wants to know if you would be interested in coming up in the booth during the first part of the game to do the broadcast with them. I've talked to Tom Grieve, and we are okay as long as you are back in the dugout by the eighth inning in case we need a pinch hitter."

This was a no-brainer! In the second inning, I trotted up to the booth in full uniform and trotted back in the eighth inning. This became my routine for the rest of the season.

HSE was responsible for televising home games on cable. A short time after I began to broadcast, they asked me if I wanted to join the telecast the following year to do some selected home dates. Not only did HSE ask me, but KTVT, who did over-the-air road games, offered me a job as well. Why not? I thought I know baseball! The job was a matter of learning the tempo of broadcasting and knowing when to say what. God opened this opportunity for me in my first year after leaving the uniform. I became a television sports analyst for about 100 Texas Ranger games. Amazing! God is good in His timing!

Time and again, I have witnessed His love for me opening up an unplanned window—a form of confirmation. Sitting on the bench that day in a Rangers uniform to broadcast games in the booth is one example of my lack of planning and His brilliance in offering job cover in an area with which I was familiar and had gifting. Every time this has happened, I am in awe of his goodness! Before leaving the broadcast booth six years later to pursue a business, Steve Busby and I would be recognized as the best pro team broadcasters in the DFW area. I have discovered the value of waiting on God.

> "Let waiting be our work, as it is His. And, if His waiting is nothing but goodness and graciousness, let ours be nothing but a rejoicing in that goodness, and a confident expectancy of that grace. And, let every thought of waiting become to us the simple expression of unmingled and unutterable blessedness, because it brings us to a God who waits that He may make Himself known to us perfectly as the gracious One. My soul, wait thou only upon God!"
>
> ANDREW MURRAY, *WAITING ON GOD*

Day 12 Meditation

PROMISE

> But those who wait for Yahweh's grace
> will experience divine strength.
>
> They will rise up on soaring wings and fly like eagles, run their race without growing weary, and walk through life without giving up.
>
> ISAIAH 40:31, TPT

MUSIC

Listen to ***In Control*** by Hillsong Worship.

REFLECTION

- When we feel like nothing is opening up for us, we want to move, to act. In these times, it is extremely hard to wait and trust God to move. What areas in your life do you need to hope and wait on God patiently?

_____

_____

_____

_____

_____

JOURNAL A PRAYER

_____
_____
_____
_____
_____
_____
_____
_____
_____
_____

WHAT IS THE FATHER SAYING TO YOU?

_____
_____
_____
_____
_____
_____
_____

Day 13
IT'S ALL ABOUT THE TRAINING

In a profession I was born to do, with all my skills lining up to play MLB, it's incredible how difficult it was to enter and how many discouraging moments I experienced.

All of life is about training. Active forces are moving against your purpose, forces intent on bringing harm to your legacy. It is in these moments of contradiction when you feel the "push back" that you have the opportunity to choose to lean in and learn about who God is and wants to be for you.

Things did not always go as well for me as I hoped or expected, but every experience was just another part of my training. When I think back, I can see how God was teaching me to deal with adversity. I learned the most about who God is during some of the hardest times. He taught me when it was time to dig in and work hard and when it was time to rest. I'm still learning to listen better for His voice.

If I had allowed obstacles to make me quit, I would never have made it to the major leagues. I may never have made it past the field where I played as a young boy! There were plenty of times in the middle of my career when I wanted to leave baseball! But God used my moments of discouragement to reveal His purpose for me. His promise kept me going when there were all sorts of distractions trying to take me off course.

I will never forget the day of the seventh game of the 1985 World Series. The Royals had gotten behind three games to one, and they were on the verge of elimination in St. Louis before a hard-fought win in game five sent the series back to Kansas City.

It was like nothing else—a dream of significance was *so close* to being fulfilled! Game six had ended in the last inning on a slide by yours truly in what was probably the most exciting moment I ever played. It was a head-first slide to evade the tag of the late Darrell Porter, who had ventured too far in front of home plate. The Kansas City crowd went into a frenzy—my teammates and I did as well. I had to slide to the backside of the plate to avoid the tag in a thriller to force the final game. The Kansas City Royals beat the St. Louis Cardinals, and the series headed to game seven.

With just one more victory to go, the Championship was in sight. There were many family members in town for the final game, so Janet and I took the kids to spend some quiet time at one of KC's beautiful parks. I had never been so anxious as I was the day of the game of my life—and for good reason. I had dreamed about this game from the time I was caught sitting at a school desk, gazing out windows at the wrong time, catching the wrath of the teacher. I had dreamed about winning, but I had no idea how stressful the process would be! My intuition told me the game would be a blowout, but I didn't know who was going to win.

"Jim," Janet interrupted my thoughts, "what's going on in your head, where are you?" It was not unusual for me to get caught in my head during family time, but Janet had a soft gentleness in her voice, given the situation. She knew the stakes!

"I've got this crazy notion that the game is going to be a blowout," I responded. "All the other games have been so close, and I don't think anyone can emotionally handle a close final game seven to be world champs."

The words "world champs" rolled easily off my tongue. WOW! I thought, *In eight hours one team would be crowned World Champs!*

Once I got to the stadium, my nerves settled down. *Should have come earlier,* I thought. For years, I had trained myself to put my emotions on the shelf, knowing if I engaged emotionally during a game, the performance might not go well.

After the first inning, I knew if we scored one run, we would win the game—that's how good Brett Saberhagan, our young ace, was that night. By the beginning of the second inning, I was predicting a shutout. I had never seen this kid so poised, and his stuff was lights out! I conveyed my thoughts to my manager, Dick Howser, and others close by.

The Royals scored two runs in the second inning, three in the third, and then blew it open in the fifth inning with six runs! Memories of my childhood began to dance in my head—great wins in Little League, special moments with dad, and that clear memory of looking out the window and dreaming of a big World Series win.

The final score was an exciting 11-0!

We are the recipients of God's designed purpose for designated seasons. Our "working" purpose may look quite different within the scope of our lives and in a variety of opportunities in which to excel. I know I am grateful for the experiences given me to honor Him. Not all have been as exciting as the seventh game of the World Series, but each has been tremendously fulfilling. Becoming a World Champ was a great reward, but I know there is an even better spiritual reward coming.

My purpose was explored as a child through dreaming, and as a young man, those dreams turned into footprints that led me down the path of destiny. When you are locked into your purpose, today's passion will drive tomorrow's rewards.

Day 13 Meditation

PROMISE

> A true athlete will be disciplined in every respect, practicing constant self-control in order to win a laurel wreath that quickly withers. But we run our race to win a victor's crown that will last forever.
>
> 1 CORINTHIANS 9:25, TPT

MUSIC

Listen to **Shoulders** by King and Country.

REFLECTION

- World Championships are hard to get. Only through training is one put into a position to experience that kind of reward. Legacy comes down to this: in life, we are training for a victor's crown that will never wither. What crowns are you pursuing? Are these earthly ones or eternal?

JOURNAL A PRAYER

WHAT IS THE FATHER SAYING TO YOU?

Day 14
THE LONG GAME

The personal journey that leads to playing MLB for sixteen, twenty, or even twenty-seven years (as was the case of Nolan Ryan) is much harder than you might think. Nolan and I were teammates in 1989 and then worked together in the front office for the Texas Rangers. Nolan was President, and I was Senior Executive Vice-President. It was great to work for a boss you brokered into the organization!

Early in 2008, Nolan rejoined the club as President. There were many things not going well at the time, especially with the brand, and I decided to exercise a little leadership with then owner, Tom Hicks. It was a bold move because forces were fighting against the move and offered some obstacles for a short time after his appointment.

Our time together in the front office was great, with the Rangers going to the World Series in 2010, where we got beaten by San Francisco. Then in 2011, we gave the game away to St. Louis—where twice we were one pitch away from winning the title.

We had a great run for about six years and saw attendance records that, because of the seating capacity of the new stadium due to be completed in 2020, will never be surpassed. Nolan had an uncomfortable departure from the Rangers in 2013, and I stayed on for about seven months more before my exit.

One day, sitting in the lower seats behind the Rangers on deck circle, which were reserved for Nolan and ownership, we got into a discussion about our playing days. On this particular day, the topic of longevity came up. The subject of long-playing careers was important to both of us since his twenty-seven plus years were longer than anyone in history, and I had stretched out sixteen years as a catcher.

No one sets out to project a specific amount of years to play because those who make it to the Bigs know how hard it is. The average working years for a MLB player is four. But we all start out with hopes of extended playing days. Players see how often the front office sends players up and down from AAA to the big club, but most of us start by thinking, "If I can just make it through playing the entire first year in the majors, that will be great."

Once a player makes it through their first year with their big league team, the expectation changes to, "If I can just make it to four years, that would be really cool."

If you made it to four years, there was another shift in expectations: "I think I've figured some things out, and maybe I can extend this for a while if I stay healthy. If I can just make it to ten years, then I'll have the maximum allowed number of years to muster out with pension."

During that four to ten year span, the pressure to perform increases because your salary increases, and you are expected to deliver. Most of these years brought anxiety because performance has a slippery slope. The threat of not performing well enough is always hanging over your head. You work hard, and you hold on to hope with a death grip, hoping to soak everything you can out of your career!

If a player makes it to ten years, the goal then is to play as long as you can until they take your uniform away! After I hit ten years, I considered the next six years to be some of the best for me because I had a greater sense of certainty in my ability, and I had grown personally from handling pressure.

There were so many moments of insecurity in my early years of baseball. I feared losing my starting role as a catcher; I feared injury, which caused me to sign a contract too early. Then, in the middle of my career, I wanted to leave baseball and head to the mission field to do something that felt more significant. Then there were all the times I just wanted to quit because of the tremendous grind with my desire to succeed yielding to the pressure of seasonal failure.

None of that sounds like someone who was certain of anything, yet I kept holding on—which is what hope does. Hope is the certainty of knowing good things are to come, even if you can't see it in the moment. Even when assurances and talents line up perfectly with your given purpose, it is hard to walk out all the "dailies" of life. If that purpose gets sabotaged and stolen by the enemy, it becomes even more difficult.

When it comes to following your purpose, hope matters. That doesn't mean you have all the answers along the way; it means you have hope to anchor your soul in stormy seas. When purpose aligns with all peace and intersects with your developed gifts and talents, you can rest assured that good things are in store.

God plays the long game.
He never gives up on you.
He plays until you win.

Day 14 Meditation

PROMISE

> As for us, we have all of these great witnesses who encircle us like clouds. So we must let go of every wound that has pierced us and the sin we so easily fall into. Then we will be able to run life's marathon race with passion and determination, for the path has been already marked out before us.
>
> HEBREWS 12:1, TPT

MUSIC

Listen to ***Oceans*** by Hillsong Worship.

REFLECTION

- The long road of legacy is hard to navigate without help. Describe the hope that holds you in difficult hours. What keeps you going?

_____

_____

_____

_____

_____

- Is God calling you out into deep waters of trust to experience more of Him? Explain?

JOURNAL A PRAYER

WHAT IS THE FATHER SAYING TO YOU?

_____

_____

_____

_____

_____

_____

_____

When a train goes through a tunnel and it gets dark, you don't throw away the ticket and jump off. You sit still and trust the engineer.

CORRIE TEN BOOM

WHAT MATTERS MOST

How you are made is a clue to why you were made. Your unique identity is no accident. God created you with certain gifts and abilities. He put likes and dislikes into your genetic makeup and gave you personality traits which are perfectly suited to His design for you.

I just shared several stories with you that related to my passion fueling my purpose. I was born to play ball! Hopefully, some things stirred in you during these last five days as you meditated through this chapter. Now, with regards to your purpose, what matters most?

Passion is the genesis of genius.

TONY ROBBINS

Chapter Four

TROUBLE IDENTIFIED

Peace I leave with you; My peace I give to you; not as the world gives do I give to you. Do not let your heart be troubled, nor let it be fearful.

—JOHN 14:27, NIV

Day 15
TROUBLE STRIKES

I spent a remarkable number of days living in cities connected with my Major League Baseball career. There are fifteen teams in both leagues, with several having two teams (such as San Francisco, Oakland, Los Angeles, Anaheim, Chicago, and New York). Manhattan was the most enticing to me in many ways. It was almost castle-like, complete with a moat, surrounded by water on three sides.

As I add up my twenty-two years as a player, broadcaster, and executive traveling in those cities (not including all my personal travel adventures), it's a lot of days! I have lived over six months in each of twelve American League cities—nine months each in Milwaukee and Chicago, twelve months in Kansas City, and calling Arlington, Texas, my home. This doesn't include about two year's worth of days spent in spring training sights in Florida and Arizona. Half of my marriage to Janet of over forty-eight years has been separated by an MLB schedule—probably why we are still on our honeymoon!

In other words, I know big cities. I know their strengths, their temptations, pitfalls, and how to survive in them. I know what places to stay away from, how to make it from Point A to Point B, how to locate great hotels and find the best restaurants to enjoy. I almost wrote a book one time on all the great big league city restaurants. It is much easier to travel today, but I learned the art of expedition before there were mobile phones and apps to guide you!

Americans have an unquenchable thirst for more. The culture of big cities highlights this thirst because there are so many options for diversion and entertainment that it's more evident in those places. The passion for more is everywhere—the push to be the biggest, fastest, and best. There is a drive for making money, a euphoria in all the available thrills. There is a fascination with the sights—Broadway shows, landmarks sporting events, attractions, and the theatre. Everywhere you turn, there is an option to buy more stuff, and opportunities to satisfy all other kinds of desires are readily offered. But the thirst for more isn't found only in big cities. The thirst for more is a mindset. The demand for personal satisfaction and access to endless choices is everywhere, but in small towns, there is more community, and the drive for more is just a bit less pronounced.

I have noticed that many people who live in metropolitan areas want to spend their weekends escaping to places of rest. The pursuit of more amplifies the pace, the noise, the busy-ness, the confusion, the hours of work, the stress, and the proximity to so many people.

Big cities can also be great places to hide. You can put your head down and make sure not to look up, talk to no one. There are pockets of isolation and avoidance, and enticements are lurking around every corner.

This driving desire for more results in a willingness to bury emotions and sacrifice relationships with others. Though some can flee to the country when the week is over, not everyone can escape to quiet places of solitude.

Those who reside in more rural places often long to visit big cities for all the just mentioned reasons, thinking there is something better. After a few days of that intensity, however, they are usually ready to go back home! Big cities can provide exhilarating moments. It is hard not to get caught up in the lights and glimmer, but look closer, and you'll find these places are full of grind. The pace, the smog, sidewalk trash, smells, and the lack of friendliness soon wears thin. I love visiting these places, but I wouldn't want to live there. After a few days, I can't wait to get home.

When we plan to get away, we rarely choose a city. Mostly, we end up wanting to go to places with beaches or mountains. These make for the better escapes for us. In reality and without consciously being aware, our quest is really to recapture a part of the peace and rest of the Garden, in harmony with God, the Legacy Giver. This peace is lost to us in this life, but one day all will be restored. We have an undeniable desire to find peace, calm, and rest. We long for joy!

Day 15 Meditation

PROMISE

> No test or temptation that comes your way is beyond the course of what others have had to face. All you need to remember is that God will never let you down; He'll never let you be pushed past your limit; He'll always be there to help you come through it.
>
> 1 CORINTHIANS 10:13, NIV

MUSIC

Listen to *My Deliverer* by Chris Tomlin.

REFLECTION

- Do you feel caught up in the rat race, pushing yourself to earn more, have more, and achieve more? Has this led you to a place of compromise with your priorities or in conflict with key relationships? In what ways?

  _____

  _____

  _____

  _____

- Don't beat yourself up. We all fall prey to this trap. Know that God is capable of delivering you out of a mess. Will you trust Him today? Where are you in need of His deliverance?

  _____

  _____

  _____

  _____

Our heart is on a quest to recapture the peace and rest of the Garden.

JOURNAL A PRAYER

WHAT IS THE FATHER SAYING TO YOU?

Day 16
NO MISTAKES

Everyone in the family learned to love spring training; it was a great starting place for the long baseball season ahead. Florida and Arizona offered terrific places to spend six weeks together every spring. Florida had the beaches, and Arizona had the dry air with places close by to take mountain hikes. The beauty was incredible. Our kids still talk about their love for spring training and the time our family shared building legacy.

Spring training offers the best environment for a veteran player to prepare for the regular season. Rookies and others trying to make the team will grind it out daily during training, but for the experienced player, it's a great time to get the body in shape, establish your swing in your time, review defensive skills at your position, get to know your new teammates, and leave early to enjoy the area with your family.

An even better way to view spring training is how it mirrors grace in relationship with the Father. A rookie player is nervous, always fearing they will get cut from the team. The rookie is worried about keeping their spot on the team. A veteran player (or, in our parallel, the beloved) can't really make a mistake big enough to cost them their position. Wrongs are forgiven for those pressing to get ready for the regular season. In life, the beloved also cannot make a mistake big enough to keep them from a life beyond this land in the spiritual realm. The veteran baseball player experiences a comfort level, knowing he is valuable and accepted. The beloved believer can have the same.

TROUBLE IDENTIFIED

In training, it is all about grace. You are there to learn and practice to acquire the skills to succeed. You are there to grow, to get better, and to conquer obstacles in your path. In Jesus, rookies always make the cut. The moment you accept Him, you become a beloved veteran. You are valuable and accepted and cannot be cut from the team. We are all in training together, all working out the kinks in this land, preparing for something better!

You are part of the beloved.
You are highly valued by God.

Day 16 Meditation

PROMISE

> There is therefore now no condemnation for those who are in Christ Jesus.
>
> ROMANS 8:1, NIV

MUSIC

Listen to **Give Me Jesus** by Jeremy Camp.

REFLECTION

- Given the scenario comparing spring training for the veteran player to the Christian life, how does this affect you? Does it give you some relief and make you want to praise God?

JOURNAL A PRAYER

WHAT IS THE FATHER SAYING TO YOU?

Day 17
SKILLED OPPONENT

In pro sports, you are keenly aware that there is a talented opponent who is out to beat you. At the major league level, opposing teams send out their best scouts to record a player's strengths and weaknesses. Their sole intent is to target vulnerabilities. Meetings take place with many attending all with a singular purpose: to beat a player and defeat his team. There is no difference in the spiritual realm.

Beating your opponent and winning the victory is the whole point of baseball. During the '85 World Series against the Cardinals, we were in game seven—the deciding game. We were at the end of the fifth inning and leading 11-0. The game was ours. We knew we were champions if we could just stay the course. Playing those last innings was the most fun ever!

My biggest dream was about to become a reality. I was so close I could taste it! From my past experiences, I had learned that in the middle of success is when you are most vulnerable to letting down your guard, making careless mistakes, or bad choices. We celebrated between every inning. Teammates and I would run up into the locker room to watch the national networks set up for the post-game celebration, and it added to the euphoria. We were laughing, giving ourselves high fives, and every other action successful athletes perform in those moments. But when we arrived back in the dugout, it was serious again. Why? We knew we had a great adversary in the other dugout and didn't want to give them any edge in the fight. Teams that make it this far have an amazing ability to rebound and gain momentum.

We remained alert, never letting our guard down or our level of play diminish. I wanted a shut out. I had no desire to give the Cardinals any encouragement for a comeback—not one run! They put up a good fight and gave no more runs to us, either. The score remained at 11-0 until the end.

I have likened the last four innings of game seven of the '85 World Series to a relationship with God. The victory of eternity with Him is ours; we know the outcome in advance. Knowing the end from the beginning makes a difference in the way we live life now with all its benefits, of which, joy and peace are central. But your adversary is waiting for an open window, a wrong choice, careless actions through which he will take full advantage.

Conceit driven by an unchecked thirst can twist something that God intended for good and His glory. Our choices are important, and they matter to our relationships and our legacy. We know we have the victory, and this is worthy of celebration. However, we must never let our guard down and give our adversary an opening to rally.

TROUBLE IDENTIFIED

Day 17 Meditation

PROMISE

> The thief comes only to steal and kill and destroy; I have come that they may have life, and have it to the full.
>
> JOHN 10:10, NIV
>
> Therefore put on the full armor of God, so that when the day of evil comes, you may be able to stand your ground, and after you have done everything, to stand.
>
> Stand firm then, with the belt of truth buckled around your waist, with the breastplate of righteousness in place, and with your feet fitted with the readiness that comes from the gospel of peace. In addition to all this, take up the shield of faith, with which you can extinguish all the flaming arrows of the evil one. Take the helmet of salvation and the sword of the Spirit, which is the word of God.
>
> And pray in the Spirit on all occasions with all kinds of prayers and requests. With this in mind, be alert and always keep on praying for all the Lord's people.
>
> EPHESIANS 6:13-18, NIV

MUSIC

Listen to ***The War is Over*** by Josh Baldwin.

REFLECTION

- We have a very skilled opponent fighting against us. It cannot be fought with our own ability but with spiritual weaponry, clothed with the full armor of God. Take an inventory of your spiritual armor. What pieces need attention? Identify any strongholds in your life that need to be turned over to Jesus for victory.

JOURNAL A PRAYER

WHAT IS THE FATHER SAYING TO YOU?

Day 18
A TIME FOR COURAGE

In 1975, Billy Martin's Rangers were playing a game in Minnesota, and I was catching for my childhood hero, Ferguson Jenkins. The previous year he was 25-12, making Fergie a 7-time 20-game winner in Major League Baseball. He is now a Hall of Famer. He didn't need me to call a game but graciously affirmed me in post-game comments.

In the middle of this game against the Twins, the bases were loaded, and the count was 0-2 (no balls, two strikes). Billy hated hitters getting a hit with the count 0-2, especially with fastballs thrown. On every 0-2 count with every pitcher, I had to stand up and step out from behind home plate to the side opposite the hitter to get the pitcher's attention. Then I had to go through the motion with my throwing hand displaying the 0-2 sign with my fingers.

This action was silly with Fergie, and he was getting agitated about it, but I decided I would rather have him disturbed than Billy! Martin also hated a hitter getting a hit in a crucial situation unless a curveball was thrown. Veteran players on the team who knew Billy as a player said it was because he couldn't hit a breaking ball. (Nice strategy!) Thus, I learned how to call a game during my first eighteen months in the show. I now get a kick out of youth coaches calling pitches for their young catchers. From my perspective, these guys would be better off flipping a coin.

Now, back to the game! We were in a crucial situation, 0-2 count, bases loaded with two outs when I moved into a squat. Fergie was already agitated with the 0-2 thing when I signaled for a curveball. Fergie shook me off. What? Oh no! I thought, the perfect storm was seconds away. It was a 0-2 count—a crucial situation—a must to throw a breaking ball. I flashed another curve ball sign, and Fergie was stirred up even more with the Billy curve ball thing. He started his windup without the next sign; I would clearly have no say in the next pitch.

Fergie threw a fastball and in the middle of the plate (not typical for him) where the ball got hit past him into centerfield, driving in two runs. If I had the weather apps I have today, they would have shown maximum torrential downpour in a matter of seconds. I heard bats and helmets flying in the dugout. I used my mask and glove to camouflage my glance to our dugout, where I saw Billy on the top of the dugout, veins popping, shouting non-edifying words at me! I knew I would take the blame.

When the inning was over, there was a temptation to go to the Minnesota Twins dugout and ask their manager, Gene Mauch, if he needed a catcher. But I knew he already had a good catcher in Butch Wynegar.

When I made it back to the dugout, Billy jumped me with unbelievable wrath. For the first time in our relationship, I shot back in his face and bellowed, "I didn't throw the pitch, Fergie threw it, go talk to him!"

Immediately Billy fell back in shock; there was a slight moment of silence as he pondered his next move. His eyes pinched tight with anger, then he shouted, "You're out of the game! Go down to the end of the bench and sit!"

When a major league player is taken out of the game for any reason, the general protocol is to go to the locker room and take a shower. No, not this time! I had to stay in the dugout at the other end from Billy getting showered with his fear-laden glances, intimidating and shameful smirks from the top of his castle steps in the dugout.

When I casually entered the locker room after the game, I noticed everyone else quickly vacating into other areas. Everyone, that is, except Billy, Rangers President, Dr. Bobby Brown, and Rangers Owner, Brad Corbett. All the players were moving fast from the locker area while Billy and Bobby were face-to-face screaming at each other. As I took a couple more steps into the locker room, Billy said, "I want to send Sundberg to the minors."

"You'll send him down over my dead body!" came Dr. Brown's response.

Eventually, all my teammates returned from the atmosphere of smoke, shame, and blame to their lockers. I didn't get sent to the minors. Around mid-season of '75, within ten days of the scene between us, Billy was fired.

The enemy is the accuser of the brethren. He throws his weight around, intimidates us, and is always threatening to diminish us. It takes courage to withstand what the enemy throws at you. Under pressure and amidst accusations, God gave me the courage to stand fast. That lesson has remained with me to this day. God is my defender. My courage comes from His care.

You cannot swim for new horizons until you have the courage to lose sight of the shore.
— WILLIAM FAULKNER

Day 18 Meditation

PROMISE

> Be on your guard; stand firm in the faith;
> be courageous; be strong.
>
> 1 CORINTHIANS 16:13, NIV

MUSIC

Listen to **You Make Me Brave** by Amanda Cook.

REFLECTION

- Have you ever been assaulted by a boss or leader? Have you ever endured false accusations? This is not fun! Shame is often a tool used to manipulate a person into the desired action. Shame causes us to feel small and unworthy, fearful for our reputation, angry or bewildered. Whether you are the one who feels shame or the one who has made someone else feel ashamed, how would you consider addressing this issue?

_____

_____

_____

_____

_____

JOURNAL A PRAYER

WHAT IS THE FATHER SAYING TO YOU?

Day 19
ISOLATION'S INVITATION

Between the ages of eight and ten, I had a couple of negative experiences that occurred with my dad, causing the wheels to come off our relationship in my Land of Innocence. The event would haunt my ability to grow emotionally and develop healthy relationships for many years.

The fact that I loved riding my bicycle must have been a precursor to how much I now love riding my Harley. One morning during the summer, I was working on my bike with a wrench when it slipped from my hand and hurt my thumb.

Out of my mouth shot, "Sunny Beach!" Those were my exact words (though my internal expression was somewhat different)! Almost as fast as I said it, I ducked my head and looked around for my dad, in fear that he heard.

I would later find out from my grandmother that the reason dad hated cussing was that her father cussed like a sailor, among other embarrassing things my great grandfather did in front of my dad. So, dad grew up with a grandfather who consistently shamed him with his words. This was emotionally unhealthy for him, and as a result, he determined that no child of his was going to grow up using foul language. Not a bad thing to have, and I am thankful for the result today.

However, as a kid, I was less thankful for the lesson. After raising my head slightly, I saw dad coming out from around the corner of the garage. It was a summer day and not the Fourth of July, but I was on the verge of seeing fireworks in the daytime.

TROUBLE IDENTIFIED

"What did you say?" blurted my dad.

"I said sunny beach, you know, dad, like a sunny day at the beach ..."

My quick thinking and creativity were not received well. Dad picked up my sturdy ten-year-old frame, my feet never once touching the ground, as he opened two doors and threw me on my bed. He then proceeded to wail on me in a way I had never before been disciplined.

Discipline for bad behavior is a good thing, but this was over the top. I really don't even know today what was going on in my dad's life at that time to set him off in that way, but it had major ramifications on me that would last into my adult life. I don't think he would have done this had he known the damage it would do to me.

In the middle of taking the licking, I was weeping, and I asked Howard (no longer dad, but someone less personal), "What did I do that was so wrong?"

His response would forge a message inviting emotional isolation in me for too long a time. "Jim," he answered, "it's not what you said; it's what you were thinking!"

Looking back as a ten-year-old and after years of intermittent counseling, let me now interpret how I took Howard's (my dad's) comments. "Jim, I don't care what you think, I don't care how you feel, keep that stuff to yourself, and never screw up again or else!"

So, I went into emotional isolation with the fear of screwing up, driving me deeper into a dark pit, unable to open up relationally to anyone. Even as an adult during a high profile Major League career, this early encounter was still causing me harm.

I got punished not for what I did, but for what I was thinking. I love my dad. It's incredible what dads or moms can do to someone, and yet that connection between parent and child is still pursued by the child until the abuse has its last words and families become irreconcilably broken.

This incident drove my fear of being transparent and affected my ability to be honest with emotions or genuine in developing loving relationships. This cycle lasted years and actually thwarted my ability to lead others well until the traps were exposed, and the voice of shame was denied its accusations.

Most of my early adult life, and throughout my MLB career, I struggled to overcome negative messages which came from a variety of childhood fears. Most of these were irrational and crippling, bordering on the edge of paralyzing. During the off-season, I was inactive and had more time to think about things. Fear had more play in those times. Thinking gave way to isolation, where I hid from things I didn't want to face—these times of brooding led to panic attacks. There were days I was unable to leave my house. Few knew this, and my baseball persona would make it hard to believe, but it is true. I know firsthand the paralysis of fear and anxiety.

Fear and its partners, shame and blame, were real to me. I know them well. They drove me to emotional isolation and created damage to my relationships. Incidents from our childhood often open areas of fear, doubt, and shame that can affect us our whole lives if not surrendered to Jesus. But there is a path to freedom, and I found it! I found a way to confront fears embedded in my childhood, which threatened my purpose, threatened to steal my legacy.

You, too, can find the path to defining freedom.

Imagine your life without fear. Imagine if you were free from all the negative "What if?" scenarios playing out in your mind. Scenarios like "What if I drive at night and hit a deer and die?" or "What if I buy a pool, but a child drowns?" What sort of joy would you be kept from if you worried about "What if I get a boat and someone gets hit by the propeller?" These things will likely never happen, and there is no amount of insurance you can purchase to protect you from the "What ifs?" in life. Abstaining from reasonable behavior for fear of what might happen is precisely what the enemy of your soul desires to do—rob you of joy, rob you of the expression of purpose and steal your legacy.

My occupation forced me to confront my issues. There was nowhere else to go. I'm thankful because I'm not sure working through my stuff would have happened unless given such a passion for playing and my desire to push through to the other side. The baseball arena was my field of play to work out my issues. It was the amphitheater where I would eventually come to know my courage, find my internal grit, and diffuse the fears. My desire to play at the highest level and succeed at what I was "called to do" was a more passionate plea than that of folding to my fears.

Courage doesn't happen when you have all the answers. It happens when you are ready to face the questions you have been avoiding your whole life.

SHANNON L. ALDER

Day 19 Meditation

PROMISE

> The Lord is my revelation-light to guide me
> along the way; he's the source of my salvation
> to defend me every day. I fear no one!
>
> I'll never turn back and run from you,
> Lord; surround and protect me.
>
> When evil ones come to destroy me, they
> will be the ones who turn back.
>
> My heart will not be afraid even if an army rises to attack.
> I know that you are there for me, so I will not be shaken.
>
> Here's the one thing I crave from God, the one thing I seek above all else: I want the privilege of living with him every moment in his house, finding the sweet loveliness of his face, filled with awe, delighting in his glory and grace.
>
> I want to live my life so close to him that he takes pleasure in my every prayer. In his shelter in the day of trouble, that's where you'll find me, for he hides me there in his holiness.
>
> He has smuggled me into his secret place, where I'm kept safe and secure—out of reach from all my enemies.
>
> Triumphant now, I'll bring him my offerings of
> praise, singing and shouting with ecstatic joy!
>
> Yes, listen and you can hear the fanfare of
> my shouts of praise to the Lord!
>
> PSALM 27:1-6, TPT

MUSIC

Listen to ***He Knows My Name*** by Francesca Battistelli.

REFLECTION

- What are the "What if's" paralyzing you?

  _____
  _____
  _____
  _____
  _____
  _____

- There is a way out! You must learn to identify your emotions and understand from where they come. Take some time to think through what sets you off in anger or fear, or isolation? Now, what does it look like for you to take your next step toward freedom?

  _____
  _____
  _____
  _____

JOURNAL A PRAYER

WHAT IS THE FATHER SAYING TO YOU?

Day 20
JUST DO IT

When I was ten and out in the park looking for baseballs one morning, I heard tires squeal. Looking up to see what was making the noise, I witnessed a car hit a man on a motorcycle and throw him screaming into a bush. The man on the motorcycle later died.

The vivid memory and sound of that moment as a child would come back whenever I decided to get on a friend's motorbike. Though I liked the idea of riding, once on a bike and moving down the road, the vision of that childhood memory replayed—it was a looping clip in my brain. Fear would soon take over, and I would quickly return the bike.

By 2012, I had pushed through many fears, and I had come to an exceptional understanding of the best way to diffuse fear. I would pray. Then, I would do whatever was making me fearful as often as I could until the spirit of fear was gone! So, I bought a Harley and prayed and rode until I had no more fear of motorcycles. Knowing what I had learned about overcoming fear, I bought a bike and never looked back. It's one of the most amazing, fun things I do. I may die on a bike, but I probably have a greater chance of dying in a car or falling down stairs or any number of ways to go. Death is certain; joy is a choice. I am currently the proud owner of my third bike. The Holy Spirit loves riding it with me.

Fear is a prison to which we hold the keys!

Day 20 Meditation

PROMISE

> For the Spirit God gave us does not make us timid, but gives us power, love and self-discipline.
>
> 2 TIMOTHY 1:7, NIV

MUSIC

Listen to ***How Glorious*** by Anna Byrd.

REFLECTION

- What is something that fear is keeping you from?

  _____
  _____
  _____
  _____

- What would help you conquer that fear and just do it?

  _____
  _____
  _____
  _____

JOURNAL A PRAYER

WHAT IS THE FATHER SAYING TO YOU?

WHAT MATTERS MOST

This chapter highlighted how our soul has an enemy, and how that enemy wants to steal our identity and thwart our purpose. He comes with lies to accuse and condemn us and keep us from walking in fellowship with the One who created us and calls us His child.

Think over times when you know the enemy has fought against you. What matters most when confronting fear?

Chapter Five

TASTE OF THIRST

"For I will pour water on the thirsty land, and streams on the dry ground; I will pour My Spirit on your offspring, and My blessing on your descendants."

—ISAIAH 44:3, NIV

LEGACY PLAYBOOK

Day 21
PRIORITIES

Veteran baseball fans never tire of Billy Martin stories. Everyone I meet seems interested in hearing about Billy Ball! There are more stories about him than I have room to share, but I want to share another with you.

In the year and a half I played with Billy, there were at least a half dozen times when I would come into the locker room after a game and experience total chaos with Billy right in the middle of it! He would scream insults at the top of his lungs. It was not uncommon to hear things hurled at you like, "How can you call yourselves big-league players? How can you eat after that kind of performance? You all stink! None of us will have a job if you keep playing like you did tonight!"

As usual, I was the last to enter the locker room following the game. I first had to collect all my catcher's gear, and I liked to take a short post-game breather to reflect on my performance before heading inside with the rest of the team.

One night, I could feel the tension before I even opened the door. I slowed my pace, listening, then I slithered into the locker room as quietly as possible. Without Billy's notice, I took the seat nearest to the door and listened to another five minutes of his rant—verbal abuse spewing from his mouth.

I heard everything he said, but all I could think about was food. The game was over … we lost … move on. I was ravenous since the last time I had eaten was around 2:00 pm, and now it was 10:00 pm. All the post-game meal, which had been so nicely prepared and placed on a table in the middle of the locker room, was now on the floor. Billy had wiped all the food to the carpet, punctuating his disgust with our performance.

Only the bravest of us would think about dipping into the exquisite delicacies remaining on top of the bigger piles that had not yet touched the floor. The stench of the carpet's surface (after all, it was a locker room) was a powerful deterrent. But I, for one, was patiently waiting for the kill. I eyed the piles of food as my stomach growled, waiting for the last word to be uttered, all the while I was strategically thinking about my approach. I'm going to eat, I thought, period!

Finally, Billy flung his final shot, "The way you played tonight makes me want to vomit! How can you eat?!" he threw his arms above his head, ripping his baseball cap off for emphasis, and then he left the room.

I watched him closely. Okay, I thought, please go to your office and vomit so we can eat!

I had only a slight hesitation before moving to select the best of the best. This kind of scouting report only comes with experience, and I was a qualified observer. I was determined to win the hunger games!

My teammates who knew me and also loved to eat were all watchful—eyes toward each other, surveying the food on the ground, and keeping watch on Billy's office all while jockeying for position for the buffet spread out all over the floor.

We must have looked like vultures hovering over fresh roadkill! Sure, we had just taken a beating on the field by the opposing team and in the locker room by our coach, but no amount of shame was going to foil our post-game mission that day!

TASTE OF THIRST

Day 21 Meditation

PROMISE

> This is why I tell you to never be worried about your life, for all that you need will be provided, such as food, water, clothing—everything your body needs. Isn't there more to your life than a meal? Isn't your body more than clothing?
>
> MATTHEW 6:25, TPT

MUSIC

Listen to **Love of My Soul** by Lauren Dunn.

REFLECTION

- Priorities are an essential part of life. What subject matter grabs your attention? What pursuits energize you?

  _____

  _____

- I know today's story was humorous and focused on my physical hunger after playing a ball game, but the parallel applies to destiny. If you are hungry enough, you won't let the accusations of your soul's enemy keep you from reaching for the prize. What are you hungry for? What are you willing to wait for and seize opportunities because the benefit is greater than the challenge?

  _____

  _____

JOURNAL A PRAYER

WHAT IS THE FATHER SAYING TO YOU?

Day 22
MY WAY

Most of my life, I never really promoted myself anywhere in any position. This wasn't humility on my part; it was because I had a poor image of myself and struggled believing I was good at what I did. It never seemed to be easy wherever I journeyed to perform, but somehow I always finished with good results.

After a short break from twenty-two years in MLB, I returned to the sport with the Rangers in 2002. Coming back after a few years of absence was a grind to re-establish credibility in the world of baseball. I did, however, reach a period where momentum picked up, and I was promoted three times in a short period without ever asking. I just responded, "Yes!" to the invite of the President of the Rangers, Jeff Cogen.

After several years with the Rangers, the day came when I wanted more influence in the organization. I knew I had a handle on the team's needs, so I went to Jeff Cogen's office. Basically, though nicely, I threatened him saying, "If you don't promote me to a place of greater influence, I'm going to leave." This was the first time I had proactively pursued a promotion—ever! Later, I was promoted to Executive VP of Public Relations and Communications before finishing as the Senior Executive VP under Nolan Ryan.

So, by 2007, I had a beat on the organization and how to make the Rangers better. I eventually brokered Nolan Ryan to the organization, among other changes. But the road was more difficult and overwhelming than I anticipated. I often felt overwhelmed and outmatched by corporate politics.

Though there were many obstacles to overcome, my tenure with the Rangers was good in the beginning. Earning two American League Championships certainly paved the way. However, in our last six years with Nolan Ryan, we experienced only about six months of peace.

Nolan left the Rangers in the fall of 2013. I continued until June 2014 before leaving without any recognition of accomplishment. I pursued promotion, and even with its upside, that promotion placed me in a position where I was in over my head. Ultimately, I landed in a bad spot. Doing things my way turned out to be not such a good idea.

Know your limitations and be content with them. Too much ambition results in promotion to a job you can't do.

RICKY GERVAIS

Day 22 Meditation

PROMISE

> Do nothing out of selfish ambition or vain conceit. Rather, in humility value others above yourselves, not looking to your own interests but each of you to the interests of the others.
> PHILIPPIANS 2:3-4, NIV

MUSIC

Listen to **Losing My Religion** by Lauren Daigle.

REFLECTION

- Have you ever done things your way? How does that typically work out?

  _____
  _____
  _____

- Is there a better way? What would that look like?

  _____
  _____
  _____

JOURNAL A PRAYER

WHAT IS THE FATHER SAYING TO YOU?

Day 23
CHASING

Through most of my years as an MLB player, I chased hard after things I grew up believing would quench my thirst. I was making more money than I thought possible, traveling the world, winning awards, accomplishing much in position, and more. Having less might have resulted in shaping me to be more relational and healthier emotionally.

Though I learned to play in the big arena, I actually loved sandlot ball better. In the Majors, I ran toward things—accomplishments, titles, power, position, authority, money, and whatever might satisfy my thirst or heal my heart. I attempted to erase the damage to my esteem over never being good enough, enduring harsh disciple, and abuses of all kinds. Emotional isolation was my standard defense, and reaching a destination became more important than the journey. Chasing hard helped me ignore the reality of my wounds.

To enjoy the journey is an attempt to enjoy God in the moment. He lives in the moment, not somewhere down the road. To run hard towards an accomplishment is to get in front of God for personal gain, personal gratification, and seeking glory without Him. However, no matter what you achieve, it is only an illusion of significance. It's not the real thing.

Sometimes running hard enough from my bad experience of the past covered the wounds with ambition and busy-ness. I know that less than would look different to me today in terms of assets and things acquired, but my time to build a lasting legacy with Him would be more significant. Ambition is an intoxicating lure and hard to balance without intimacy with the Father, Son, and Spirit. Unyielded ambition creates only a more unquenchable thirst.

As a result of my drive to ignore my past and chase an illusion of significance, I ended up moving outside of healthy operating boundaries. I bought into a culture filled with ways to operate alone. Occasionally, with my back against a wall, I would make unauthentic pleas for help, playing games with God like He was some type of Santa Claus to grant my wish at the moment to relieve my pain. In other words, I was a poser.

At times, I ran in front of God's design for me, seeking things without Him while He patiently waited for me. There were days of guilt for not grinding it out, for not running hard enough toward an idol. I didn't believe God had the best for me; I felt like I needed to look out for myself. I was a self-provider, self-comforter, self-seeker. Our culture's message today is to believe we can do things better—just do it! But this message is one of false hope. The problem with thirst goes all the way back to the Garden. Thirst is written into our fallen nature!

Most of us are guilty of running hard after the wrong things. We are driven, unable to rest, exhausted from seeking more when a little less is healthier. We find temporary reprieve by things that don't bring lasting comfort, only momentary release. We isolate ourselves from reality. Our families are broken. In an effort to slake our thirst, we destroy important relationships and cut ourselves off from the only One who can satisfy.

> *A paradox of the soul is that it is incapable of satisfying itself, but it is also incapable of living without satisfaction. You were made for soul-satisfaction, but you will only ever find it in God.*
>
> RICKY GERVAIS

TASTE OF THIRST

Day 23 Meditation

PROMISE

> Come to me, all you who are weary and burdened, and I will give you rest. Take my yoke upon you and learn from me, for I am gentle and humble in heart, and you will find rest for your souls. For my yoke is easy, and my burden is light.
>
> MATTHEW 11:28-30, NIV

MUSIC

Listen to **Spirit Move** by Kalley Heiligenthal.

REFLECTION

- What are you chasing, and is this healthy for you and your family?

  _____
  _____
  _____

- What would it look like if you released this to God and allowed Him to quench this thirst?

  _____
  _____
  _____
  _____

JOURNAL A PRAYER

WHAT IS THE FATHER SAYING TO YOU?

Day 24
QUEST FOR THE BEST

In July 1978, I was on the front cover of *The Sporting News* with the headlines reading, "Best Backstop?" I had just come off my best six months of baseball occurring over two seasons. I would never duplicate the feat again. From the end of June '77 to the first of July '78, I hit over .330 and won another Gold Glove in a series of six with a second of three All-Star trips.

I had much to be happy about, but the truth is, I was miserable inside after getting there. The journey was the best part; the arrival left me empty. I had always dreamed about being the best, and I practiced hard, showed up early, stayed longer than anyone else, visualizes all day hitting the opposing pitcher that night. Everything I did was geared toward that goal. And during all this, I was the most non-relational, self-centered scared person around. After this incredible run of public accomplishments, I couldn't imagine being able to do it again. After a brief enjoyment, thoughts of "why?" and "what for?" propelled my thinking. My desire for significance was now beginning a true journey of discovery.

I would be at home with the family and sitting around the dinner table, but I was not there relationally. To be the best at anything causes you to sacrifice the most important things. My drive to be the best at baseball caused me to ignore being the man I needed to be for my family and friends.

It is exhausting to be at the top. There you find a bottomless pit of self-reliance. The enemy will try and steal the pure beauty of anything and distort its appearance into something counterfeit. The thirst that led the charge for me was euphoric and an illusion—it had to be to muster the energy needed to remain at the top. My single focus was directed toward the need to be the best. My desire to chase after the illusion of satisfaction left my life parched with emptiness in the long run.

Everybody wants to replace you or criticize some aspect of your game. Ask anyone at the top of their field—CEOs, scientists, doctors, actors, musicians—someone is gunning to take your place. The top is a lonely place because while everyone wants to be your friend, you keep everyone away. After all, you know they will likely be gone in a flash.

The ability to achieve the same excellent performance year after year takes more than my talent offered. It required more than I was willing to sacrifice. The real benefits were not worth the struggle for me. There was no lasting emotional reimbursement to refill what was drained away. "Do it again, Jim" "Then do it again and again and again …" The pressure was unbearable. Fame was not a lasting benefit but a quick fading memory. Happiness called out from deep, but could not be realized.

There was a voice deep inside me wanting to be heard, but I kept it locked down, afraid of what might happen if I let it out. Of chief concern was a fear that I would be punished. That fear drove me to isolation. Then one day, the voice crying out would no longer be silenced by isolation.

Recently, I've run into kids who don't know Nolan Ryan. That's almost sacrilegious in baseball—especially in Texas! I've found others who don't know who Ivan Rodriguez is. Some of you may even have to Google their names right now! Fame is fleeting. It does not last.

Yet, somehow, we keep chasing the illusion of satisfaction, and we embrace its euphoric message. The voice of our accuser whispers, "You need to do more to get what you want. You need to do better in order to be satisfied. Being the best is the right way to go. More is what you need. More is what you must have. More is better, and you are not good enough without it."

I had my moment in the sun. Receiving recognition for being at the top was exciting, but the price tag was too high. Looking back, I wish I had better known my Father. I wish I had known what lasting legacy looked like so I could have pursued Him much earlier in my life.

Day 24 Meditation

PROMISE

> It's true that I once relied on all that I had become. I had a reason to boast and impress people with my accomplishments—more than others—for my pedigree was impeccable.
>
> Yet all of the accomplishments that I once took credit for, I've now forsaken them, and I regard it all as nothing compared to the delight of experiencing Jesus Christ as my Lord! To truly know him meant letting go of everything from my past and throwing all my boasting on the garbage heap. It's all like a pile of manure to me now, so that I may be enriched in the reality of knowing Jesus Christ and embrace him as Lord in all of his greatness.
>
> PHILIPPIANS 3:3, 7-8, TPT

MUSIC

Listen to ***Lay it All Down*** by Will Reagan and United Pursuit.

REFLECTION

- Have you ever wanted to be the best at something? If so, what sacrifices did you make? Did you have to compromise?

_____

_____

_____

_____

- Looking back, what would you do over if you could?

_____

_____

JOURNAL A PRAYER

_____

_____

_____

_____

_____

WHAT IS THE FATHER SAYING TO YOU?

_____

_____

_____

_____

_____

_____

*Fame is fleeting.
Popularity is temporary.
But character creates a legacy
and integrity is eternal.
Seek the higher things.*

BRYAN FOSTER

Day 25
AIN'T NO SATISFACTION

Are you old enough to know the song, *Satisfaction*, by The Rolling Stones? In the mid to late 70s, I began struggling with awful depression. Initially, I didn't know why or how it was happening. It was confusing, to say the least. Long before counseling was acceptable or popular, I began seeking help to weather the storm. Over the next twenty years, there would be four seasons of counseling before past dysfunctions were healed. Other than a few who were closest to me, no one knew my struggle. Today, most teams employ a sports psychologist or psychiatrist to ensure the mental well-being of their players. It's a no brainer. But back then, the need for a counselor was seen as a weakness, and one had to keep it in hiding.

Since it was not "hip" to venture into an office for a counseling appointment, I made sure I was conveniently five minutes late, so all the other people waiting for an appointment had suitably vacated the waiting area before my arrival. My backup plan was always to hide behind dark sunglasses—just in case there was a lingering fan or two who might recognize me. Many people in the DFW area thought the Texas Rangers were a law enforcement group, so I felt a little safer. Wearing a baseball hat was out because most people knew me better with it on. A Rangers cap would give me away for sure, and I was scared of letting anyone see I had a desperate need.

When I was a boy of ten, I hit three home runs in a game, but my father's response had been, "Jim, if you had kept your elbow up on your strikeout, you would have it another home run." This event seared the message, "nothing short of perfection is good enough" into my heart.

The damage this created shadowed my sports legacy—as all shame and condemnation do—until the Trinity intervened in my brokenness and made me whole.

My drive to succeed was spurred by a deep need to win the approval of my dad. Before long, I also required the approval of others to feel worthwhile. The love of our earthly father is so embedded in our identity that we will do crazy things to receive it. This need drove me so hard I reached the point of self-sabotage and often lacked productivity. Eventually, this unresolved issue harmed my performance numbers during certain times throughout my career. There were long seasons where I played ball while struggling with deep depression. I can go back now and see the correlation of those times and the dips in my stats. Athletes weren't supposed to struggle. They are supposed to be heroes. We were meant to play at peak performance—strong men without emotional issues.

By the time I got to the Major Leagues, if I got a hit the first time up, then I needed to get two hits that night. If the game went long enough, two hits had to become three. No matter how well I played, I always ended the game dissatisfied. I always needed one more hit than I got to consider a perfect performance. In reality, this was unattainable. But in my mind, I was always pushing and pushing for more. All along, I was beating myself up to hit more home runs—even though home runs were not even my greatest strength as a player.

It was crazy, destructive thinking because if a player hitting in my spot in the batting order got one hit each game over the twenty-six weeks of a regular season, he would hit over .300! A player with that average would most likely be an annual All-Star and eventually become a Hall of Famer. But my thinking was warped and probably hindered my case for being an MLB Hall of Famer. I drove myself so hard to find significance. I desperately wanted to hear the words, "Son, job well done!" that I was willing to hurt myself emotionally. I pushed my body beyond the number 10 on the back of my uniform.

I caught 1,400 games in ten years while enduring Texas heat—often in the triple digits. Crazy stuff like that almost killed me. Neither before or since has anyone caught that many games in that period! Had I caught fewer games, I could have played more offense, experienced more enjoyment, and less stress. Less would have been more.

Most of my career, I was running from the hurt of a bad experience I had as a ten-year-old. I ran toward an illusion of significance that could never be fulfilled in human terms. I believed a lie that held me in bondage and turmoil.

Years later, I would at least hear the words, "Son, job well done," spoken to me by a heavenly Father whose love I cannot begin to comprehend. Oh, how I wished I had learned to hear his voice much earlier in life, but I am so grateful I finally answered His call! To find this kind of love requires that the old heart and soul are peeled away and replaced with a new heart. Only then can you receive the significance of His provision and love. It just can't happen any other way.

TASTE OF THIRST

Day 25 Meditation

PROMISE

> After looking at the way things are on this earth, here's what I've decided is the best way to live: Take care of yourself, have a good time, and make the most of whatever job you have for as long as God gives you life. And that's about it. That's the human lot. Yes, we should make the most of what God gives, both the bounty and the capacity to enjoy it, accepting what's given and delighting in the work. It's God's gift! God deals out joy in the present, the now. It's useless to brood over how long we might live.
>
> ECCLESIASTES 5:18-20, MSG

MUSIC

Listen to ***King of My Heart*** by Steffany Gretzinger and Jeremy Riddle.

REFLECTION

- Is there something from your past that hinders you in your present? Do you feel driven to have a need me that never seems to be answered? What is this for you?

_____

_____

_____

_____

- Hand that situation over to God. Ask to hear Him say to you, "Well done!" What would it take for you to replace the lie you have believed with His truth?

JOURNAL A PRAYER

WHAT IS THE FATHER SAYING TO YOU?

Day 26
PERSPECTIVE GAP

One of the most confusing events I ever attended happened in 1998, my last year in the Major Leagues. It was customary for pitchers and catchers to meet with a coach, generally the pitching coach, to strategize opposing hitters and discuss strengths and weaknesses. The purpose of the meeting was for our starting pitcher and the bullpen pitchers to gain the best advantage in getting opposing hitters out. This particular meeting, I will never forget.

Over the length of my career, I discovered the best way to conduct these was to discuss scouting reports with pitchers in small groups; the starting pitcher, the pitching coach and me, or sometimes just the pitcher and me could use our knowledge of the hitters along with the latest reports given to us by our advance scouts. I knew how to pitch guys from the first-hand experience in my head. The only information I required from scouts was data on new players who were recently transferred from the minor leagues to the majors and details on current players who were hot. I wanted to know which players were hot in case the first base was open. It might make more sense to walk them intentionally rather than give them an opening for a bigger score. Sometimes we pitched around these players with kind of an "unintentional intentional" base of balls.

I have found that the best approach to control loose cannons (who think they are experts) is to talk to them in small groups. In larger groups, the need to be impressive and be heard makes it challenging to get to the real information you need.

Our pitching staff was really struggling, primarily due to a lack of talent, so to solve the problem, our pitching coach decided to pull every pitcher and catcher into a room to sit and watch videos together on each hitter and discuss strategy. The meeting ended up in chaos!

I had been in the majors sixteen years and had never before experienced what I saw that day. As the video played, I couldn't believe the disagreements that occurred between players watching the same video. Though the evidence was right in front of them, they argued on and on about where the pitch was actually thrown.

"That pitch was inside!"

"No way, it was down!"

"Are you crazy, that pitch was right in the middle of the plate!"

"Are you blind? It was the outer half!"

It was crazy! I was the most seasoned guy in the room and had just weeks to go in my career. I walked out of the room and never listened in on another meeting. It didn't matter much since I only played one game during my last six weeks, but the confusion was beyond my tolerance.

Although everyone was looking at the same video, each person had their own angle, their own agenda. Every voice offered conflicting opinions, and we couldn't agree on the pitch location, let alone a strategy for how to deal with it. There was a total lack of unity or shared purpose—it was every man for himself.

Information is subject to as many interpretations as there are people. Perspective is vital, and in the end, there must be a reliable authority by which we "call the ball." When we hear the voice of God, we can't help but interpret what He says and means through our filter of knowledge and experience. As believers, the Bible is the final authority. Whatever we process, we must measure our motives against God's Word. We need to submit our desires to God and make sure our will aligns with His.

Day 26 Meditation

PROMISE

> What causes fights and quarrels among you? Don't they come from your desires that battle within you? You desire but do not have, so you kill. You covet, but you cannot get what you want, so you quarrel and fight. You do not have because you do not ask God. When you ask, you do not receive, because you ask with wrong motives, that you may spend what you get on your pleasures.
>
> JAMES 4:1-3, NIV

MUSIC

Listen to **God Only Knows** by King and Country.

REFLECTION

- How open are you to the perspective of others? Do you need to be right, or can you allow yourself to be taught by someone else? Why or why not?

  _____

  _____

  _____

- When you seek truth, it can sometimes seem evasive. When you go to God in prayer, do you bring Him a list of what you want Him to do in your life (and in the lives of others), or do you come into His presence and allow His Spirit to guide your prayers? If you find that your requests seem to be lingering unanswered, is it possible that what you are asking for does not align with His will for the situation? _____

JOURNAL YOUR UNANSWERED PRAYERS

_____
_____
_____
_____
_____
_____
_____

WHAT IS THE FATHER SAYING TO YOU?

_____
_____
_____
_____
_____
_____

WHAT MATTERS MOST

In this chapter, I shared several stories which revealed how often I chased the wrong things, felt driven to perfom at all costs, and did things my way. Unresolved issues from my past continually tripped me up. None of those things worked out very well for me, it left me thirsting after things which could never satisfy my longing.

It was not until I came to know Jesus that I began to understand the refreshing blessing of living water and how following God's plan yielded much more successful outcomes than chasing achievements or fame ever could. I began to learn what mattered most. What matters most to you?

> *Love casts out fear, for when we know we are loved, we are not afraid. Whoever has God's perfect love, fear is gone out of the universe for him.*
>
> — A.W. TOZER

Chapter Six

LOSS

"Blessed be the God and Father of our Lord Jesus Christ, the Father of mercies and God of all comfort, who comforts us in all our affliction ..."

—2 CORINTHIANS 1:3, ESV

LEGACY PLAYBOOK

Day 27
LOSS OF OUR BABY

In 1981, the Texas Rangers were on the last day of a road trip in Seattle when a call came into the locker room. Rangers' manager, Don Zimmer, took the call and then quickly came to my locker to tell me that my wife's obstetrician was on the phone. Since Janet was in her last month of pregnancy, I immediately jumped in alarm to answer the call.

The doctor's voice on the other end was soft and sensitive, "Jim, I'm not sure how to tell you this any other way except to say that I'm sorry." I could feel my pulse quicken, and my stomach felt sick. He continued, "Janet came in this morning with signs of labor," he paused and took a breath. "The baby went into cardiac arrest, and I'm very sorry … your baby girl didn't make it."

I was stunned. *Janet!* my heart cried out. "Is Janet okay?" I asked. *What must she be going through?* I wondered. I can't believe she's alone right now! My mind swirled. I don't know how long I stood there in silence. "Did you say, girl?" *Yes. A girl, we knew that …* I slipped back into silence; my emotions were all over the landscape of my heart.

I don't remember getting off the phone, but an eerie subconscious memory later emerged of a long, slow walk back to my locker with complete silence in the room. All my teammates were still as if caught between my news, which had quickly circulated, and their preparation for game time.

The first conscious thing I remember was the manager tapping my shoulder and asking me if I wanted to go home or stay for the game. The question itself continued my paralysis.

Many of you know what it's like to get hit with a disruptive, life-altering message—a child killed by a drunk driver, a parent's diagnosis of cancer, a friend or colleague found dead from a heart attack, and so on.

The question posed for me to choose "to return home or stay" was mind-numbing. Once I gathered my emotions and reviewed airline schedules, our team's charter flight home after the game felt like the best scenario since both options were close in departure time. The prospect of traveling with people I knew provided comfort and much-needed emotional support. *Yes, better for me,* I thought, *but maybe not really best for Janet!* I sighed, feeling uncertain.

Next, my manager posed an even more thought-provoking question, "Jim, now that you decided to stay, do you want to play or sit on the bench?" My emotions were playing mind games with me, reaching deep into places never used previously! I could delay the conflict and play the game, something I was accustomed to doing, or face it head-on and leave the team behind and head for home. Feelings challenged my innermost being for the right pathway, calling out to a deeper level I had not felt before, but I was unable to make any connections.

It was a tough situation, and I had to make a choice. I could either move through adversity in the moment or draw up in isolation. *But what should I do?* I knew Janet would spend most of the day by herself whether I caught a commercial flight or flew home with the team. No matter what, she would have to deal with the grief and pain of the loss without me. The inner conflict was uncomfortable. When I was uncomfortable, I usually opted to avoid the conflict. The choice I made that day was to stay and play ball.

Looking back now, I realize that any effort to get home earlier on my part would have made a difference demonstrating my care and concern for Janet. Even if I had arrived about the same time, had I chosen to leave the team and go to her side, it would have brought her comfort. In that season of life, however, I could not clearly see this. Heading back with the team seemed like the right thing to do, and if I was with the team, I preferred having my head in the game over the torment of grief and loss.

For the first time in my life, however, I had no desire for personal or even team success. I didn't care about a winning performance that game, and in a strange new way, it felt good. My detachment from performance meant I couldn't really lose—no matter what happened. No one would expect me to do well anyway under the circumstances, so the pressure was off. Most of the time, I cared so much and held on so tightly that the pressure inhibited me from the full release to excel.

The distraction of play was a tonic to my broken heart, but there were several moments during the game when my mask gave me the freedom to let tears flow. I couldn't hold them back, no matter how much I tried to deny what had happened. I thought by not sitting on the bench that I would dodge a bullet and not have to think about it. Instead, it was incredibly insensitive to Janet. A wrestling match ensued in my subconscious mind.

Amazing insights for the kingdom were gained for me in the 'ole Kingdome that day. I played well despite the circumstances, and we handed the Mariners a loss. It was a game-changing experience for me. It was my initial glimpse into what it feels like to release results into the calming presence of the Father. It was my first real experience in how obstacles can eventually lead to spiritual and professional upgrades.

This would begin a new place of freedom from the pressure to perform for me. In the midst of dealing with a tragedy, it provided an insightful revelation about performance.

There was such a dance with my emotions to find my way to the other side of that blow. In hindsight, I didn't stand as the head of the house. I didn't move as quickly as I could to protect Janet that day. I don't believe God cared more for my performance than He does for a man caring for his wife. But as He always does, He worked the choice I made that day for my good.

There were no immediate answers to our child's death. Time, though, can offer resolution and peace. Maybe you have experienced what an incredible miracle it is to experience when God takes a tragedy and turns your heart towards thankfulness.

Later, we were grateful for the birth and life of another wonderful daughter, and now we are thankful for a beautiful granddaughter and grandson. I would give anything to know the beautiful girl we lost, but I am thankful for getting to experience what it felt like to release results into the hand of the Father's goodness. In the end, legacy is about building a loving family and not some performance trap. His faithfulness through all my choices and in every circumstance continues to overwhelm me. What a good, good Father!

Each day we choose to live the legacy we leave.

PAM FARREL

LOSS

Day 27 Meditation

PROMISE

> And we know that in all things God works for the good of those who love Him, who have been called according to His purpose.
>
> ROMANS 8:28, NIV

MUSIC

Listen to **When We Pray** by Tauren Wells.

REFLECTION

- In the middle of a difficult season, it can feel as if things aren't ever going to get any better, but it's not over yet. Your story is not yet finished. Rest assured that God will work this situation for your good. Is there a question you need to ask God about your circumstances?

_____

_____

_____

_____

JOURNAL A PRAYER

WHAT IS THE FATHER SAYING TO YOU?

Day 28
KEEP SHOWING UP

Another dance with my emotions occurred in a more pleasant setting. It was 1987, and I was in my fourteenth year in MLB, just starting the downside of my career. I was sitting on the bench in Wrigley Field wearing a Cubs uniform. The previous years had been spent playing a crazy number of games. My body was ready to play fewer games, but my pride and ego were not yet in agreement. I was really struggling with the lack of playing time, and on this particular day, I hadn't played in two weeks. My attitude about it was terrible, but for the moment, I was enjoying talking to a pitcher friend about theology. So, now you know what Big League players talk about in the dugout!

The sun was beaming on that beautiful summer day in Chicago, and the sounds and smells of baseball were filtering over the top and into the dugout as ushers broadcast their goods. The breeze carried a hint of smokiness, and I thought how great a hot dog with mustard might be! In the pauses of our deep discussion, my thoughts drifted back to when my dad and I came to Wrigley Field to watch the Cubs play. The memories were vivid, the old reaching out to touch the present moment.

I sat with my friend, our legs kicking back and forth on a high bench—like kids watching their favorite sport. I thought I heard my name mentioned. "Scott, did you just hear my name?"

"Yes," he replied, "it looks like Gene Michaels wants you to hit!"

He hasn't the slightest clue what he is doing! I thought, *If he knew anything, he would be playing me more!* I ducked behind Scott and muttered, "You have got to be kidding me!"

My wonderful day was interrupted. My childhood memory slammed into reality. *Can't I just sit here and enjoy my contract? What is he thinking? I haven't played in two weeks, TWO WEEKS!* I felt a familiar knot in my stomach—pressure to perform. He's never used me to pinch-hit, I shook my head, *I haven't the slimmest idea how to prepare for this!* "He's an idiot!" I mumbled, while all of these thoughts rushed through my head.

I glanced down to gain eye contact, and sure enough, the manager was motioning with his finger for me to join him. "Scott," I shook my head, "I think you're right … " and my thoughts took off again, discrediting his position.

Stop it, Jim, I told myself. *Get yourself together. Show a little composure!*

I was fighting this mental battle to respond correctly, waging against the urge to complain. I felt like Gollum in Lord of the Rings. You know, the bald-headed little man who looked like he came from another planet with those awful-looking eyes and mouth. Gollum was caught between the evil power of the ring, his "Precious," and destroying it to gain his freedom.

I walked to the front of the dugout. "Jim," Gene instructed, "get your bat. I want you to pinch-hit for the pitcher."

I nodded somewhat sheepishly, but now it was time to focus on the task.

The only thing I knew about the game at this point was my great conversation with Scott and that the Cubs were playing the San Diego Padres. I didn't even know the score, much less what inning it was, how many outs, who was on base, or if anyone even was on base. I had been enjoying the summer breeze, some childhood memories, and great conversation. My mind had been nowhere near the actual game!

As I reached the manager and he motioned me to hit, I said, "Okay," then panic struck! I hadn't brought my bat into the dugout that day because I hadn't played in TWO WEEKS! Quickly, I ran up the tunnel from the dugout to the locker room to retrieve my bat from the team's bat rack, all along thinking, *He has to be the most stupid manager in baseball!* But now, I started to buffer my negative thoughts with, **Come on, Sundberg, gather yourself. Get a plan!**

I searched frantically over the rack, not able to find my bat as someone yelled from the other end of the dugout down the tunnel, "Get back to the dugout, Sundberg!" In a panic, I just grabbed a bat and a helmet and headed out.

I was met with an angry home plate umpire who had walked to our dugout to tell me, "Let's go, Sundberg, what's wrong with you?" *At least he didn't say S<u>a</u>ndberg,* I thought. He definitely was not there to ask for an autograph!

I started up the dugout steps as I attempted to quell the inner voices fighting each other. I stopped in the on-deck circle to take a few swings, loosen up, and process the game situation to make a plan. I came to the stark realization; the bases were loaded, we were in the fifth inning with one out, and we were down 6-1. Gollum returned. *Oh, that's why the manager wants to throw me under the bus. He doesn't want to waste one of his better hitters on this situation.* "Stop it, Sundberg," I said out loud, "this thinking won't get you anywhere!"

My strategy was to look for a ball up in the strike zone and try to loft it to the outfield for a sacrifice fly giving us a run. I felt okay about the plan … and then I glanced at the mound to see who was pitching. *What?!* I thought again, *I've never hit this pitcher! Doesn't the manager ever look at stats? He is the stup…* "Stop it, Jim! Just get in the batter's box and stick with the plan!"

I felt accomplished just in finding my way to the batter's box since it had been—well, you know how many weeks. I steadied myself as I looked out to the pitcher. He started his delivery and threw the pitch. With my eyes slightly open, I swatted at a pitch, up and out over the plate. POW! The ball drifted high to left field! I came out of the batter's box and was halfway to first base while I watched the ball clear the fence. **Grand slam home run!** *That's got to be the smartest manager I've ever played for in my life!*

We went on to win the game, and a month later, as an added bonus, a photographer sent me a picture of the swing with the ball in the upper left-hand corner. Today, this photograph represents for me to keep showing up no matter the emotions.

Day 28 Meditation

PROMISE

> As for us, we have all of these great witnesses who encircle us like clouds. So, we must let go of every wound that has pierced us and the sin we so easily fall into. Then we will be able to run life's marathon race with passion and determination, for the path has already been marked out before us.
>
> HEBREWS 12:1, TPT

MUSIC

Listen to ***You're Gonna Be Okay*** by Jenn Johnson.

LOSS

REFLECTION

- Having a reservoir of positive inner dialogue can be helpful when your emotions cause you to fret. What do you do when your self-talk sabotages you? How do you respond?

_____

_____

_____

Talk to yourself like you would to someone you love.

BRENÉ BROWN

- Write down some things with which you need to come into agreement about heaven's perspective of you. By stating these things without the emotional pressure of a hard moment, you can put them into your spirit. That way, the next time you are squeezed, you have prepared yourself with truth and can walk in victory!

_____

_____

_____

_____

JOURNAL A PRAYER

WHAT IS THE FATHER SAYING TO YOU?

Day 29
LOSS OF LEGACY

My great grandfather owned five farms in the mid-west before the Great Depression. He gave one farm to each of his four sons. When they came out of the Depression, they all had to move to one farm to live. It was a great loss to the family.

My great grandfather and great grandmother had been considered better off than most because of owning the farms. One of their sons was my mother's father, who became a pipe-smoking grandfather to me who adored me being on his lap.

It is my understanding that my great grandmother never forgave great grandfather for the loss of the family farms. Though they lived in the same house, they stayed in separate bedrooms in their last twenty years and never talked again.

When young, I was shown where they lived. Every time we passed the house, the tragic story of loss and non-reconciliation could be felt. Divorce was not an option back then, so their last years together were lived in isolation within the walls of their little castle. There they listened to voices that kept wounds open and offenses alive, forfeiting joy that should have been our family's legacy.

My grandfather grew up in that environment. Years of not dealing with his fears and living in shame took their toll. He never owned property again. He and my grandmother, who died in her mid-nineties, spent the rest of their lives renting apartments. That shame and regret was imprinted on my mother in different ways. Generational stuff like this needs to be recognized and spoken to proactively and with authority to keep generational curses at bay. Otherwise, they keep passing on down the line.

The Great Depression had a lasting influence on many people in that wonderful generation. While some ran and hid in fear, others used it as a stepping-stone for something better. I decided long ago I wouldn't run and hide if I experienced financial loss, which I did. Thankfully, I kept looking for the next opportunity and the next … and they always came.

We cannot change the family to which we were born. We cannot go back and undo mistakes made by our ancestors or right their wrongs. Their decisions, along with circumstances they encountered, have long-lasting consequences with regards to legacy. While we may not be able to go back in time to fix things, we can decide to embrace the blessings available to our bloodline and reverse any curse. So, with great intention, I have worked to break the generational curse of fear and shame off myself and halt it from gripping my children. I am willing to stand in the gap spiritually and restore what was lost. I desire to leave a family legacy of acceptance, grace, and joy.

Day 29 Meditation

PROMISE

> But instead, be kind and affectionate toward one another. Has God graciously forgiven you? Then graciously forgive one another in the depths of Christ's love.
>
> EPHESIANS 4:32, TPT

MUSIC

Listen to ***Living Water*** by Lauren Dunn.

REFLECTION

- What legacy has been left to you by your family?

  _____

  _____

- Is this legacy what you desire to leave to your children? Forgiving one another is imperative to creating a legacy worth leaving. Is there someone in you need to forgive?

  _____

  _____

JOURNAL A PRAYER REQUEST:

_____

_____

_____

_____

WHAT IS THE FATHER SAYING TO YOU?

_____

_____

_____

_____

Story 30
ESCAPE TO FREEDOM

Most of my first ten years with the Texas Rangers was as a player the organization would use around which to build their team. In other words, a good catcher is one of the positions needed to build a winning club.

My star status began its fade in my eighth year. I experienced a downturn of my performance as the club came under new management, and there were a couple of disgruntled pitchers who cast blame for no longer getting hitters out in my direction.

Several new people joined the team, and as the club shifted, I began to lose my status and popularity in the organization. Over the next three years, accusations increased, and blame began to take its toll. My performance suffered.

The voices of complaint against me were many and came from every direction. This chipped away at my standing. The influence I once held drained away until those making decisions no longer listened. I made a mistake. I ran and hid from the conflict, which only served to increase the credibility of those voices. But the adversity held a blessing. As the territory around me grew increasingly hostile, I began to travel to a new land flowing with God's favor.

This was the landscape in December of '82. It was a couple of weeks before the Winter Meetings when General Manager, Joe Klein, called me into his office to tell me he would try to trade me during the annual event.

I had finished the third year of a six-year play, ten-year pay contract, so there were three years remaining. The most important element of the contract was that whoever had my services during the sixth year, paid half the ten year contract (years six through ten).

In other words, all deferred money and the one remaining year of salary were all connected to the sixth year of play. Let me clarify: one year of play would cost a team five years' salary. It wasn't supposed to be that way. The original intent was for an amount of money to be deferred as each year was played. Deferred payments were designed to reduce annual federal income tax by spreading six years of earned salary across ten years of payment. The money deferred was meant to be independent of the sixth year of play, but my attorney had missed the fine print.

When Joe communicated he was going to trade me that year, I urged him to reference the contract clause of deferred payments to whatever team made the trade. I knew a club wouldn't want to be saddled with that kind of payment for one year of play. Joe acknowledged he would, but he didn't. When it was all said and done, he did not discuss the contract clause with the new team before the trade.

The Dodgers made the trade with the Rangers without looking at the agreement. It wasn't until later that the magnitude of dollars owed on the sixth year of the contract was discovered. Once the Dodgers realized the small print, they moved to offer me a new contract for a third less money than an already guaranteed—putting me in a difficult spot. Because I had a no-trade clause (meaning I had to approve any trade), I declined the offer from the Dodgers, as anyone would. In a weird turn of events, this sent me back to the Rangers, even though I hadn't really left.

The new Rangers' manager, Doug Radar, entered in 1983. There I was at his mercy with my credibility declining with the organization, and his hand to guide the finality of my ten-year tenure with the Texas Club. Those who followed my career know a little about the '83 season. Radar often discredited my character and ability, both in person and in the newspapers. It was a difficult year.

Friends and family would say to me, "Stick up for yourself, don't let him say those things that aren't true!" But it was hard enough to play the game. I didn't have the energy to engage in a public dispute and fan the flame for others to join in and pile on.

There was always someone ready to hurl insults and assault me while I was trying to make a living. Getting into it with them would only increase the volume of their voices. Back then, it was just live or in the papers. Now, the phenomenon of social media amplifies this even further!

In the back of my mind, a verse of scripture was paraphrased in my memory. It kept coming to me, "Let it be. I'll take care of it. I will raise you up at the right time." Somehow, I knew God would take care of the situation—and me. Indeed, He did! But there was very little to feel good about during the '83 season as Radar seemed bent on making sure I wouldn't want to return to the Rangers for '84.

The few years of wrestling with my faith had opened a greater acceptance of His presence in my life. So, in the winter of '83, I was traded to Milwaukee for what I call "A Year of Recovery." Within a one-year period, great things happened to me; spiritually, professionally, and financially.

Eventually, Radar was fired from the Rangers. Not long after that, he was again fired from the Angels. He would never again return to MLB. Within one year of the trade to Milwaukee, the Texas Rangers were insisting on my return to the club. Instead, I opted for Kansas City in '85 and eventually won a World Championship.

God fought my battle. As I opened myself up to Him, I escaped the prison of accusation. The more I embraced kingdom-thinking, the greater advancement I experienced.

LOSS

Day 30 Meditation

PROMISE

> No weapon that is fashioned against you shall succeed, and you shall confute every tongue that rises against you in judgment. This is the heritage of the servants of the Lord and their vindication from me, declares the Lord."
>
> ISAIAH 54:17, ESV

MUSIC

Listen to *Take Courage* by Kristene DiMarco.

REFLECTION

- What battle are you facing that you need to relinquish and let God fight on your behalf?

_____

_____

_____

_____

For the Lord your God is the one who goes with you to fight for you against your enemies to give you victory.

DEUTERONOMY 20:4

JOURNAL A PRAYER

WHAT IS THE FATHER SAYING TO YOU?

LOSS

WHAT MATTERS MOST

This chapter focused on the impact of loss and the importance of perseverance through storms. Grit and tenacity are an important part of the equation, but not the whole picture. The other factor for navigating hard times is learning to trust God—not only that He has a plan and a purpose, but also that the timing is also in His very capable hands.

We all have seasons of difficulty when it seems like nothing works out the way we planned. When you face trials, what matters most to you?

_____

_____

_____

_____

_____

_____

_____

_____

_____

_____

_____

Success is to be measured not so much by the position that one has reached in life as by the obstacles which he has overcome.

BOOKER T. WASHINGTON

Chapter Seven

GAME-CHANGING LENS

"See what kind of love the Father has given to us, that we should be called the children of God; and so we are."
—1 JOHN 3:1, ESV

Day 31
A MORE LASTING APPROACH

From the time I was young, I identified with something popular or cool. I wanted to be a Major League Baseball player very early. My heroes were Roger Maris and Mickey Mantle of the NY Yankees, Ernie Banks, and Billy Williams of the Chicago Cubs, and there were many more. In fact, all my idols were players, and I had grandiose dreams of becoming just like them. Later in life, whenever I would meet one of them, I would gush all over them like I was still a kid!

In high school, I wanted to drive, or at least be associated with, a nice car—like a green '69 Chevy SS 396. Just saying those words bring back fond memories. My next goal was a good-sized brick house for starting a family, to wear certain name brand clothes with the right logos, and so on. It was the culture in which I lived. I saw myself through those windows. I attended church, but identifying with church stuff was not on a priority. Going to church was a socially acceptable religious activity.

Every step toward MLB life seemed to offer another way to identify myself that came easily and went even more easily. These fads had no staying power. I wanted to be well-liked, so I grabbed on to fashion trends by which I could be distinguished, having my first signature bat and glove, etc. But nothing matched walking onto a MLB field in a MLB uniform for the first time. Who could not get warm and fuzzy about that? Years later, I would come to realize that "something" I could not stop thinking about or chasing was an idol. I would learn that "things"—even nice ones—were not something to get caught up in, but back then, baseball was king—my little "g" god.

I spent all of 1974 playing on the same MLB fields where I had once dreamed about making an appearance. A major highlight was the awe-inspiring feeling of walking into the dugout and seeing Yankee Stadium for the first time. Who could not let this environment get all over them and define their identity? What I did for a living became who I was. It was the lens through which I saw myself. Outside of playing baseball, I had no clue of my identity as a person. So, how I performed dictated whether or not I looked kindly upon myself. This was not an emotionally healthy habit!

Over the years, I had played on a lot of terrible teams who had learned how to lose. While with them, learning to lose became easy. It's not a good thing to view yourself as a loser, but it was easy to get caught in that rut. Learning to win is a better thing to learn, especially when winning is easy. I found that once I was out of that rut, the best way to stay out was how I saw myself. I wanted to be a champion, so I began to view myself as a champion. Indeed, at last, I got a chance to experience myself through the lens of a champion, and it was great! But let me tell you, nothing compares to seeing yourself as the Father sees you through the lens of Jesus. When you catch a glimpse of your identity through His eyes, you will never again be the same.

O Holy Spirit, descend plentifully into my heart. Enlighten the dark corners of this neglected dwelling and scatter there Thy cheerful beams.

SAINT AUGUSTINE

Day 31 Meditation

PROMISE

> But those who embraced Him and took hold of His name were given authority to become the children of God!
>
> JOHN 1:12, TPT

> And you did not receive the "spirit of religious duty," leading you back into the fear of never being good enough. But you have received the "Spirit of full acceptance," enfolding you into the family of God. And you will never feel orphaned, for as He rises up within us, our spirits join Him in saying the words of tender affection, "Beloved Father!"
>
> ROMANS 8:15, TPT

MUSIC

Listen to **When You Walk Into the Room** by Bryan and Katie Torwalt.

REFLECTION

- How do you view yourself? What words or phrases come to mind when you think of yourself?

_____

_____

_____

- Do these edify who you are as a child of God?

JOURNAL A PRAYER

WHAT IS THE FATHER SAYING TO YOU?

Day 32
GAME-CHANGING LENS

The first time I heard, "Who in the world do you think you are?" was not intended to be a question of identity to be answered, but rather to be belittled, dressed full length in shame. This question can either help you express a healthy image or cause you great harm, depending on the spirit in which it is presented to you.

While visiting my oldest daughter, Audra, and her family in Rogers, Arkansas, my eldest grandchild wanted to go to a restaurant nearby in downtown Bentonville. I asked Kaleb, "Why do you want to take me there for lunch?"

"I want to show you something, Papa," he replied.

When you move about your day asking God to give you eyes to see Him and ears to hear Him, be ready. I had no idea the magnitude of what was about to happen. But since I love my grandson and really enjoy Mexican food, the trip to Bentonville was a no-brainer.

We entered the restaurant and sat down at a table close to stacked cases of Coca-Cola® bottles with some scripting in Spanish. Kaleb proceeded to pull out his phone, and from an app, projected his camera lens toward the bottles directing me to take a look. Kids know apps. I had no clue there was something even like that available.

When I looked through the lens of the phone, all the writing on the Coca-Cola® bottles was now in English. I jumped back and then looked from the side of the phone—Spanish lettering. WHAT!? I went back and forth to the phone, English … Spanish … English … Spanish. I was trying to believe what my eyes saw. The lens of my mind was trying to relay something to the beat of my heart. What message was tugging deeper, pulling me closer? As much as my eyes were telling the truth, my mind and heart were grasping for its hidden meaning. And then it hit me!

As I sat with my grandson and family pondering what I had just viewed through the lens of the phone in the Mexican restaurant, the message blew me over like a strong gust of wind. "Jim, this is how I see you as your Father—in the image of Christ." The back of Kaleb's phone was crimson red, my viewing side was white as snow, and in between was the One. God sees me through Jesus. The message was clear: THIS IS WHO YOU ARE!

Day 32 Meditation

PROMISE

> For He knew all about us before we were born and He destined us from the beginning to share the likeness of his Son. This means the Son is the oldest among a vast family of brothers and sisters who will become just like Him. Having determined our destiny ahead of time, He called us to Himself and transferred His perfect righteousness to everyone He called. And those who possess His perfect righteousness He co-glorified with His Son!
> ROMANS 8:29-30, TPT

MUSIC

Listen to **Mention of Your Name** by Jenn Johnson.

REFLECTION

- God sees you through the lens of Jesus! How does this make you feel?

_____

_____

_____

JOURNAL A PRAYER

_____

_____

_____

_____

_____

_____

_____

_____

WHAT IS THE FATHER SAYING TO YOU?

_____

_____

_____

_____

Day 33
SAVED BY GRACE

By now, you know some of my story. I was raised in a blue-collar family with our needs barely met. Baseball was a world promising future glory, and my dad's desire caused me to draw hope from the experience. My dad lived his dream through me. He was well-meaning, yet made some mistakes, as most fathers do. Anger, along with verbal abuse, the trap of identity being tied to performance, the harshness of discipline, and enduring sexual abuse from a neighborhood boy caused me to become lost in a world of confusion and despair and solidified my need for future healing.

Messages from those around me growing up, both inside and outside the home were, "Jim, if you make it to the Major Leagues, that's what life is all about!" I set my sights on this. I knew if I played MLB, my dream would be fulfilled; I would make more money than I anticipated; I would have fame, success, prestige, and all that comes with these things.

The problem was that four years into my career, I had all that plus a wonderful wife, a great home, two beautiful kids ... and I was miserable. How could that be? It wasn't about them or anyone else; it was about me—the condition of my heart. I had everything I wanted. Everything, that is, except the most important and central part of life and legacy. I didn't have a relationship with God through Jesus!

I was in a Toronto hotel room in '77 after playing the Blue Jays on a Saturday afternoon. I was reading Hal Lindsay's book, The Late Great Planet Earth. While reading a section on "being left behind," I peeled off my bed and dropped onto my knees and sobbed. I confessed my need for God and desire for a more enjoyable life—and so a page was turned. The new quest began.

There would be great moments of abundance, but there were many childhood wounds that would need healing while navigating new opportunities. These wounds affected how I responded to new obstacles like the loss of our baby and a financial hit from a good Christian friend and dealing with my relationships afterward. My emotional immaturity especially manifested in insensitive arguments with Janet and the mishandling of obstacles I faced during my career. Athletes aren't expected to be emotionally mature, and often get a pass from fans.

I have come a long, long way in my healing. I have a deeply personal relationship with the Father. And still, I am aware that most likely, some lingering pain from my past will rise up as I face other phases of life, and once again, I will face new opportunities to work through difficulties while waiting to see how God works these for my good.

I can tell you this: the decision I made in Toronto that Saturday was the stabilizer of my life and affected those I influenced around me. That decision saved me from me. From that day forward, there was no turning back. This was my motivator, no matter the obstacles!

———• • •———

If God had wanted me otherwise, He would have created me otherwise.

JOHANN WOLFGANG VON GOETHE

Day 33 Meditation

PROMISE

> For it was only through this wonderful grace that we believed in Him. Nothing we did could ever earn this salvation, for it was the gracious gift from God that brought us to Christ! So no one will ever be able to boast, for salvation is never a reward for good works or human striving.
>
> We have become His poetry, a re-created people that will fulfill the destiny He has given each of us, for we are joined to Jesus, the Anointed One. Even before we were born, God planned in advance our destiny and the good works we would do to fulfill it!
>
> EPHESIANS 2:8-10, TPT

MUSIC

Listen to **Call on Jesus** by Nicole C. Mullen.

REFLECTION

- What is your story for when you gave your heart to Him?

_____

_____

_____

_____

_____

JOURNAL A PRAYER

WHAT IS THE FATHER SAYING TO YOU?

Day 34
SEEING GOD THROUGH THE WOUNDS

Even after my conversion experience in Toronto, at times, my wounds kept me from living out my faith authentically and with authority. It was hard to hear well when the accusations from my hurts drowned out the voice of the One leading me through the healing process. As I began to heal, however, the negative voices began to subside. They did try, from time to time, to reemerge and hinder my progress, but I had more fight in me now, and would always make a comeback. As the voices dissipated, the Master's voice became more defined and clear.

The emotions wrapped around these wounds kept me on a roller coaster of doubt. I knew I was saved, but I often felt unworthy and unsure about my salvation—a significant legacy inhibitor. Addressing wounds is paramount to legacy. There is no power in your life as a believer without the assurance of salvation.

Wounds inhibit your ability to trust in others, but even more importantly, they keep you from fully trusting God. I used to think God was like my father, as many do when there is a lack of love in an earthly model. A poor earthly father relationship can be a false echo of God's love and a faint copy of who He really is. I struggled greatly with this thought until the Word and the Spirit washed over my heart to renew my thinking. It took years to root out some of the reasoning because of my dad's harsh temperament.

Early in my conversion, there were times when I recall being afraid to trust God with my deepest hurts and fears. I would not ask Him for help! I remember thinking, "What happens if God really can't help me with this? Maybe He is a lot like my dad …"

I seemed to be on a mission to find another way to heal. God was more of a backup plan, and I lived with the fear that if God couldn't help, who or what could? It scared me that if God didn't work out, then I did not have a safety net. Finally, I thought, who better than Jesus? There was a strange comfort in the thought, though it makes no sense to me today. It seemed to make sense then, to save God's participation for the last resort if everything else failed. A lie had hi-jacked my thinking and, for years, hindered my progress to heal.

There were times I didn't know how to explain the confusion I felt. Sometimes I would wrestle for months, struggling with pain and unchecked emotions. All the while, mad at myself because I was struggling. In the most difficult of times, I seemed somehow to place one foot in front of the other long enough, that one day I looked up and saw something different. I couldn't explain it then, but now know how to communicate today. God is always at work. Even in the places of confusion and helplessness, God is moving. I didn't know it at the time, but when I look back, I can see that He was there with me, working things together for my good.

God shows up big time whenever He is invited! Once I realized trust worked, I no longer needed a backup plan. Once I asked him for help, healing began. I began to trust in the thought that something good was coming from something painful. I began to understand that the hardest difficulties could have the greatest rewards. In reality, I began to believe obstacles were not something to fear but a good thing; they were something that leads to a higher understanding of who God was and wanted to be in my life.

Day 34 Meditation

PROMISE

> "He Himself bore our sins" in His body on the cross,
> so that we might die to sins and live for righteousness;
> "by His wounds you have been healed."
>
> 1 PETER 2:24, NIV

MUSIC

Listen to **You Will Always Be the One** by Loving Caliber.

REFLECTION

- When was the last time you invited God into your situation? What happened?

  _____

  _____

  _____

- If it hasn't worked out yet, it is probably not over. God is at work. Now. In your situation. Look back, where can you see His hand at work in the struggle you are enduring?

  _____

  _____

  _____

JOURNAL A PRAYER

WHAT IS THE FATHER SAYING TO YOU?

WHAT MATTERS MOST

The lens through which you view God, yourself, and others shapes how you relate to them and the world around you. If your perspective is warped, then your relationships will be warped also.

In the devotionals presented in this chapter, I revealed the shift of my perspective and how that affected my ability to trust God, to trust myself, and to trust others. Think about the lens through which you experience life and write down what matters most about this?

_____

_____

_____

_____

_____

_____

_____

_____

_____

_____

_____

Chapter Eight

A NEW PERSPECTIVE

"The Lord is not slow to fulfill His promise as some count slowness, but is patient toward you, not wishing that any should perish, but that all should reach repentance."

—2 PETER 3:9, ESV

A NEW PERSPECTIVE

Day 35
EYES TO SEE

Around the age of forty-two, we were on a trip to Colorado when I experienced a reduction in my eyesight. It was evening, and even though there was an overhead light, when I looked at a map, I noticed it was slightly out of focus. I rubbed my eyes to take another look, but my sight did not improve. Since then, my eyesight gradually grew worse. As many have experienced, I went through many pieces of eyewear and even had two surgeries in an attempt to compensate for the loss of vision. Eyesight is incredibly important.

There is an interesting scientific phenomenon that benefits a pitcher when a hitter is attempting to hit a baseball. As the ball approaches the home plate area, the mind takes over for the eyes to track the ball through the hitting zone. (The hitting zone is where the bat is supposed to contact the ball.) As the ball approaches this zone, the hitter's eyes can no longer see the ball, so the mind finishes the flight path of the ball and the hitter swings where he thinks the ball will be.

This is the primary reason why it's so important for a pitcher to have a late-breaking pitch—because the eye can't track it, and it changes so quickly that the mind cannot track it, the pitcher has the advantage. Nature gives this advantage to him.

As much advantage as a well-trained pitcher with a late-breaking pitch has over a batter, as a believer in Jesus, you have much more advantage. Walking in the supernatural affords you great benefits, even in the ordinary, everyday issues of life. As you move about your day, ask God to give you eyes to see Him at work around you. Ask Him to show you what neither your eye nor your mind can see!

Day 35 Meditation

PROMISE

> Blessed are the pure in heart,
> for they will see God.
>
> MATTHEW 5:8, NIV

MUSIC

Listen to **Son of David** by Ghost Ship.

REFLECTION

- How in tune are you to the supernatural realm? Write about a time when you saw God at work in or around you.

_____

_____

_____

_____

_____

_____

JOURNAL A PRAYER

WHAT IS THE FATHER SAYING TO YOU?

Day 36
FAVOR

One of the benefits of being a high draft choice is the favor that comes with it. I've been on both sides, and believe me; it is far better to be lavished with honor than it is to be stripped of one's dignity.

Generally, a top draft pick in pro sports has the red carpet rolled out for them. People are looking out for your best, treating you as if you are royalty. The affirmations coming from those at the top have put their credibility on the line by selecting you over someone else, placing you with the right team to succeed, giving you grace to fail, plotting a great future with you, and so on, is an incredible esteem-validating experience. It feels so much better to be on the side of conquering than it does to trudge through life feeling like a victim.

But even if you have that top-flight experience, time goes by. People forget why they picked you, and the honeymoon soon comes to a close. You no longer feel the love! In fact, the very people who put you on that pedestal are often the same ones to pull you down.

Know this: you are always God's top draft pick! He selected you before you were born; before the foundations of the earth, He called out your name. You are royalty. His affirmation of you is based on Him, not you—not your performance, not your mistakes, not even your successes. God's love is unchanging, unending, and unconditional. Wrap yourself in this truth today.

Favor cannot be achieved.
Favor must be received.

A NEW PERSPECTIVE

Day 36 Meditation

PROMISE

> For you bless the righteous, O Lord; You cover him with favor as with a shield.
>
> PSALM 5:12, ESV
>
> For the Lord God is a sun and shield; the Lord bestows favor and honor. No good thing does He withhold from those who walk uprightly.
>
> PSALM 84:11, ESV

MUSIC

Listen to **Good and Loved** by Travis Greene and Steffany Gretzinger.

REFLECTION

- Do you sense the favor of God? As God's child, He loves us beyond belief. Take a moment to ponder His favor in your life. Express your gratitude here, pour out words of thanksgiving to God.

_____

_____

_____

_____

_____

JOURNAL A PRAYER

WHAT IS THE FATHER SAYING TO YOU?

Day 37
THE UNCERTAINTY OF PERFORMANCE

During the early part of my baseball career, I struggled to hit big-league pitching. My tenure in the minor leagues was only one year, starting in Double-A before advancing to MLB the following year. I got there quickly because I could catch and throw better than most, but I had to learn to hit against good pitching while the team took advantage of my defense.

In those first three years, my identity as a player became "a no-hit, great fielding catcher." I had trouble shaking this off for most of my career, even after I began to hit well. My significance as a player was like a series of emotional ups and downs, and I was never really certain how long I would get to play. Eventually, I made it sixteen years, but I never really believed I would make it that long.

When identity is based on performance, then the way you view yourself becomes a roller coaster. You ride the highs and lows of how you perform. You are never sure of your significance, never satisfied with your accomplishments. I never made much headway against seeing myself but through the window of performance until many years later, when I met the author of identity. It was then where the obstacles I encountered became opportunities to grow in kingdom thinking.

I had been caught in a performance trap, stuck in a spin cycle of disappointment and insecurity. It wasn't until I learned to ask the Father, "How do You see me?" and "Who do You say that I am?" that I began to unhitch my identity from my performance or achievements. When I began to see myself through God's eyes, everything changed!

Day 37 Meditation

PROMISE

> Lord, I passionately love You and I'm bonded to You,
> for now You've become my power!
> You're as real to me as bedrock beneath my feet,
> like a castle on a cliff, my forever firm fortress,
> my mountain of hiding, my pathway of escape,
> my tower of rescue where none can reach me.
> My secret strength and shield around me,
> You are salvation's ray of brightness shining on the hillside,
> always the champion of my cause.
> All I need to do is to call to You,
> singing to You, the praiseworthy God.
> When I do, I'm safe and sound in You.
>
> PSALM 139: 1-6, TPT

MUSIC

Listen to **Church (Take Me Back)** by Cochren and Co.

If our identity is our work, rather than Christ, success will go to our heads, and failure will go to our hearts.

TIMOTHY KELLER

REFLECTION

- Are you caught in a performance trap unable to see the real you? How do you know this?

  _____

  _____

  _____

- What would it take to break free and connect with how God sees you?

  _____

  _____

  _____

JOURNAL A PRAYER

_____

_____

_____

_____

_____

_____

_____

WHAT IS THE FATHER SAYING TO YOU?

_____

_____

_____

_____

_____

_____

_____

> *Your real, new self (which is Christ's and also yours, and yours just because it is His) will not come as long as you are looking for it. It will come when you are looking for Him.*
>
> C.S. LEWIS

A NEW PERSPECTIVE

Day 38
HEALING EMOTIONS

Most of my early counseling experiences were spent in just giving a voice to my pain. In other words, I didn't have a language to express my emotions. At age 28, I went to my first counseling session. I was sharing something hurtful about my dad towards me, and the counselor asked me a question that dumbfounded me. He said, "Jim, how did that make you feel?"

I looked up at him, startled. I had no idea how to answer him, and I felt like I had just been asked to spell a foreign word I had never heard. I shrugged my shoulders and replied, "Can you give me an example of what you mean?"

It was like I was a young child going through a chart showing different faces communicating emotional responses with the "feeling words" written underneath. The counselor said to me, "Does it make you sad, Jim?"

I broke down and began to weep. Yes, it did make me sad. In that moment, I knew what sad felt like. This was something that, had I known at the age of ten and had the freedom to express, would have actually made me healthier along the way. But I had been programmed as a kid-robot to play pro ball, not feel feelings. Even though I loved baseball, I had never been given room to express emotions that were not tied to winning.

Over the years, more "feeling words" were added until I became very good at understanding and touching my emotions. Until you understand this fundamental principle, healing cannot happen.

There was a pastor (now friend) who helped me with the next phase of healing. He encouraged me to journal and ask the Father in Heaven what He thinks. I hadn't been one for writing, and I thought at the time that this was a strange request. I had nothing to lose and needed to feel better about myself, so I gave it a try.

It was a struggle at the onset. But before long, my requests to the Father on paper began to come back at me with words that brought life. I learned that words spoken to another are so important because they can either breathe emotional death or life. Journaling what I heard the Father say to me was an exercise in breathing life.

The process was simple. First, I wrote out, "Dear Lord," and I would write something down. Then I wrote, "Dear Jim," and sat quietly, waiting for Heaven's response. Deep in my spirit, there was a voice saying, "Keep coming to Me. Keep showing up in this place, no matter the frustration, and you will receive much from Me."

Later on, I would come to a critical understanding; God wants a relationship, and He wants that relationship to be interaction back and forth. A baby first learns to hear and understand words, then respond to what they hear long before they ever speak. If this same principle is in play with our relationship with God, then it could take some time between first hearing, then understanding, and finally responding to Him. Hearing is a fundamental part of a relationship with Jesus.

I can't tell you how much easier it is for me to hear God today. Actually, it's become a mental discipline of the spirit to help shape my heart and mind—the process of sanctification after conversion. All along, waiting for the Spirit to respond with all His brilliant answers.

In an earlier entry, I told you about an incident from my childhood when I was beaten by my father, "Not for what you said but for what you were thinking." I came away never willing to tell anyone what I was thinking or feeling again out of fear of punishment! This memory is what made me so sad that day in the counselor's office. I had no words to express the sorrow from this incident that caused me such grief over the years.

A few years ago, I took this practice of journaling and combined it with something I learned at a couple's Quest in Lake City, Colorado. I found a quiet place and journaled this question:

"Dear Lord, this is such a hurtful, confusing, and scary memory—to be beaten not for what I did but for what I was thinking! Where were You in that memory?"

This is His answer to me as I wrote it down in my journal:

"Dear Jim, I was lying there next to you! I was holding you with My arms wrapped around you! I had ahold of your heart with one hand while holding your neck and head with the other to cushion the blows. I felt every thrust, every hit, and every blow from your dad. Even then, I had a hedge around you. I felt and tasted his wrath. I buffeted you from further damage. I wept with you. I'm so sorry you had to go through that. I was so close that your tears rolled across My heart as a future memory of this moment so that I could bring you to complete healing in this season of time. You can grieve it, My son! You are safe with Me now!"

As I was receiving and writing those words, I wept for fifteen to twenty minutes. I sat there with the sun warm on my face and an internal picture of Jesus holding me in His arms. There was no better way for me to grieve, no other way to healing for me than through such a life-changing experience. It was a catalytic event that gave me the image of keeping me close to HIS heart.

At another time I wrote these words:

"Dear Lord, I don't want to leave this place of comfort. I want to stay in this moment of warmth. It feels so good, such rest ever-present. How wonderful it feels to be safe in Your arms with my grief!"

The right questions to ask seemed to come to me as much as the answers. It was almost like He was driving the entire conversation like He had been waiting longer for this moment than I had ever anticipated. I wrote more:

"Lord, it was so confusing to me, so painful. I didn't understand dad's rage. I was so afraid of him …"

He answered me:

"Dear Jim, I knew where his rage and anger came from. He was acting out of his own fear and pain. He did not know what he was doing! Your dad did not know Me, nor did he pursue Me. But I will use that terrible experience, that unjustified act of punishment to bring you newness as only I can. Others will benefit from this, My dearest son."

Healing comes in stages. God takes us as far as He knows we can go, then allows us to stabilize until we are ready to go deeper with Him. One morning as I spent time with Them—the Three-in-One—I shared fellowship on a level I had never experienced before. I wrote:

"Dear Lord, I'm ashamed to show my emotions and hurt! I want to get it all out—all the shame, all the hurt, and all the ugliness of that moment occupying my heart. I don't want to be angry anymore, Lord, I want to release it to You and forgive dad. I want my memory of that moment reflecting You being next to me, holding and keeping me in

A NEW PERSPECTIVE

Your arms. No longer do I want to see myself as a victim to the shame and hurt and punishment of that incident and let the enemy tell me lies about myself and about You. I never want to doubt Your love for me again. I would request, as Your son, for You to replace any negative thoughts about this moment with your Kingdom thoughts about who I really am and who You really want to be for me."

I sat in silence, waiting to hear. The answer flowed:

"Dear Jim, you are My courageous one! Made in my image. I knew you long ago. You have everything available that I have available to ME, all that the Kingdom has to offer. I laughed aloud when you were standing by your bike and said the words, "Sunny Beach!" It was so creative of you to say a negative word with such a funny expression. You did nothing wrong; there is nothing wrong with you. You are not a bad person. I gave you some of MY creative, active mind. I would love to see you use it in positive ways. Let Me take you there!"

And so my friends, here we are together many years later! When the words of the last paragraph were written, I was healed. There was a shift in my heart. I felt it! I occasionally read these words to remember from where I came, and they can always bring tears of joy and thanksgiving when I revisit them.

The peace that came from writing with Him is what we all thirst for in this world, an intimate connection with more than just a Healer.

I can't tell you what God would say to you in your situation. There are other circumstances much worse than mine. I will tell you that if you can muster the courage to go there with Him, be ready for something that will rock your world—something once impossible made possible.

Hope is a song we sing; it is our anthem. So, if you go to the places of darkness with Him to bring light, be ready to receive everything He wants to give you.

There is something about giving your pain a voice and dealing with wounds in the presence of the One who made you, along with the support of others, that brings you into an understanding of love, value, significance, and the certainty of knowing who God is and wants to be to you. God's love-grip of assurance embraces you like a warm blanket on a crisp, clear, cold day while sitting beside a perfect campfire.

Day 38 Meditation

PROMISE

> God, I invite your searching gaze into my heart.
> Examine me through and through;
> find out everything that may be hidden within me.
> Put me to the test and sift through all my anxious cares.
> See if there is any path of pain I'm walking on,
> and lead me back to your glorious, everlasting ways—
> the path that brings me back to You.
>
> PSALM 139:23-24, TPT

MUSIC

Listen to **Gadol Elohai** by Joshua Aaron.

REFLECTION

Today, let's do something a bit differently.

WHAT MEMORY DO YOU NEED TO ASK THE FATHER ABOUT?

_____

_____

_____

_____

_____

_____

_____

_____

WHAT ANSWER DID HE GIVE YOU?

_____

_____

_____

_____

_____

_____

_____

_____

O God, I have tasted Thy goodness, and it has both satisfied me and made me thirsty for more.

I am painfully conscious of my need for further grace. I am ashamed of my lack of desire.

O God, the Triune God, I want to want Thee; I long to be filled with longing; I thirst to be made more thirsty still.

Show me Thy glory, I pray Thee, so that I may know Thee indeed. Begin in mercy a new work of love within me.

Say to my soul, "Rise up my love, my fair one, and come away." Then give me grace to rise and follow Thee up from this misty lowland where I have wandered so long.

A.W. TOZER

A NEW PERSPECTIVE

WHAT MATTERS MOST

As I shifted the lens through which I viewed my life, I was opened up to an even greater opportunity. I began to ask God to help me see things through His eyes—to experience supernatural wisdom, favor, and blessing. A whole new world opened up for me as I learned to look through the eyes of Jesus.

When it comes to experiencing the world through the eyes of your heavenly Father, what matters most?

God is most glorified in us when we are most satisfied in Him.

JOHN PIPER

Chapter Nine

OBSTACLES TO OPPORTUNITIES

I will lead the blind by ways they have not known, along unfamiliar paths I will guide them; I will turn the darkness into light before them and make the rough places smooth. These are the things I will do; I will not forsake them.

—ISAIAH 42:16, NIV

LEGACY PLAYBOOK

Day 39
BELIEF SYSTEMS

I grew up believing challenges were a problem—something to avoid. Because of unresolved pain, this pattern of thinking was an obstacle hard to overcome. I've made great strides in adjusting these thought patterns, and now turning obstacles into opportunities is really as easy for me as making a choice: am I a victim or a victor? Difficulties shape our character, and they come with spiritual blessings and benefits. When a problem leaves me feeling rejected, I remember to look at it as God does. It isn't personal; it is just a course correction. If I stay the course and try some other angle or approach, something will eventually get better.

At the core, our belief system is developed around being either a victim of our circumstances or making a decision to rise above them. The theory is as old as time. Your gut-level approach indicates the strength of the belief system from which you operate. These attitudes become family traits that are handed down.

You have likely heard the story about a woman who always cut the end off a ham before baking it. One day her husband asked her, "Why do you cut the end off before baking a ham" She replied, "That's how my mother always did it."

At the next family gathering, the man asked his mother-in-law, "Why do you cut the end off the ham before baking it?" She answered, "I don't know; that's the way my mother always did it."

A call to grandpa in the nursing home revealed the answer, "That was because your grandmother's pan was too short to hold a whole ham."

Neither woman had ever stopped to consider if their behavior was wise or even if it made sense. They repeated the pattern of behavior of their family because that's the way it had always been done. It is important to question whether there is a better way in which to respond when confronted with challenges and obstacles.

I saw obstacles as roadblocks and not as an avenue for rewards or kingdom thinking. In truth, I have learned that challenges present opportunities for upgrades—better emotional health, greater wisdom, more spiritual benefits, and sometimes even financial rewards (though not my focus).

The reason I couldn't escape a label of a "no-hit, great fielder" was because at the time, even though I was a Christian, I was unaware of how much my pattern of thinking kept me bound. I was trapped in a belief system created by abusive parenting. My wounds of the heart had kept me captive to victim thinking. This was not conducive to breaking away from thinking I was less than I really was. This attitude probably kept me out of the Cooperstown Hall Of Fame. It was not until my sixties that I began to realize the power and authority of Kingdom thinking—viewing myself as God does. I promise you; it is a much better way to view the world!

Sometimes adversity is what you need to face in order to become successful.

ZIG ZIGLAR

Day 39 Meditation

PROMISE

> Yes, feast on all the treasures of the heavenly realm and fill your thoughts with heavenly realities, and not with the distractions of the natural realm.
>
> Your crucifixion with Christ has severed the tie to this life, and now your true life is hidden away in God in Christ.
>
> And as Christ Himself is seen for who He really is, who you really are will also be revealed, for you are now one with Him in His glory!
>
> COLOSSIANS 3:2-4, TPT

MUSIC

Listen to **More of You** by Hillsong Young & Free.

REFLECTION

- In an honest evaluation of your response to obstacles, do you generally see yourself as a victim of circumstances, or do you approach from the attitude of a victor? Why do you think this is?

_____

_____

_____

_____

- What is your attitude concerning God's power? Do you believe you are more than a conqueror through Him? How is this demonstrated in your life?

JOURNAL A PRAYER

WHAT IS THE FATHER SAYING TO YOU?

Day 40
GOD IS AT WORK

Two events occurred in the early eighties, and one more happened in recent times that fortified the principle of turning obstacles into opportunities for me. I wrote about one previously when Janet and I lost our baby girl while I was scheduled to play a game in Seattle.

Prior to Seattle, my approach to playing baseball bordered on idol worship. I was trapped in an unhealthy fear that drove me to perform. Of course, it is important to do well and apply the principle of hard work, but there is a better way. I was gripped by the fear of failure. Every thought during the day and every action during a game was driven by this fear. Because this fear consumed my thoughts, performance became my idol. Weirdly, I was worshipping that fear—it was my little "g" god. This idolatry distracted me from more important things like being in the present in my relationships with family and others.

The decision to play the game that day with no internal pressure to deliver a perfect performance turned an obstacle (the loss of our child) into an opportunity (to be free from fear of failure). I know this sounds odd, but when I decided to play instead of sit on the bench in grief, it was the first time in my life I didn't care how I performed or whether or not the team even won the game. Tears dripped down my face from behind my catcher's mask, hiding my grief. We won that game, and I delivered one of my better performances. Free from fear, I played without that hindrance. It took incredibly unsettling news to jolt me out of my thought pattern, interrupt my belief system, and allow an opportunity for me to experience joy in the game without fear of failure and the pressure to perform that fear created.

We will never know how our lives would have been changed by the baby girl we lost, but within two years, Briana was born. Thirty-six years later, she invited Janet and me to an event where I spoke to a group to bring a word of encouragement. While speaking, it struck me the event would never have taken place without Briana's birth. Briana married Stefon, and now we have a wonderful granddaughter, Brynley, and grandson, Liam—miraculous!

I may never understand this side of heaven why we lost our little girl, but I can tell you that my fear of failure took a major hit that day, I never played another game with the old mindset. Something in me shifted that day, and the tragedy turned into triumph.

Day 40 Meditation

PROMISE

> For when the ropes of death wrapped around me and
> terrifying torrents of destruction overwhelmed me,
> taking me to death's door, to doom's domain,
> I cried out to You in my distress, the delivering God,
> and from Your temple-throne You heard my troubled cry.
> My sobs came right into Your heart and
> You turned Your face to rescue me.
>
> ROMANS 8:29-30, TPT

MUSIC

Listen to **Freedom Hymn** by Austin French.

REFLECTION

- Have you ever experienced something really difficult to face, but later saw God's hand of mercy working through the hardship? Write about that time.

JOURNAL A PRAYER

WHAT IS THE FATHER SAYING TO YOU?

Day 41
WINDOWS

Another incident came several months after the birth of Briana, and God continued to show us what He is capable of doing through bad situations. I was fresh off a horrific 1983 season with the Rangers' manager. I endured much verbal abuse from him as he made every effort to make sure I didn't want to return for the 1984 season. If you think about the worst possible work environment to be in for a year, add to that the visibility of making it highly public in front of fans, that was 1983 for me.

I didn't even want to play baseball anymore after the '83 season, but my multi-year contract made it impossible to leave the game. As a result, a former college summer coaching relationship, Sam Suplizio, who had ties with Milwaukee, brokered a deal behind the scenes for me to play for the Brewers for the 1984 season. Janet and I ended up calling it the year of recovery—cooler temperatures, good environment, great teammates, and an All-Star game pick. Because of my trade clause, we even received a significant financial reward. Before the season was over, I was ready to keep playing for years ahead.

Harry Dalton, who was the general manager of the Brewers and a man I grew to respect, told me on the front end that I would only be in Milwaukee until young catcher, Bill Schroeder, was ready to take my place. I knew that could happen within a year.

Weeks after playing in the 1984 All-Star game in San Francisco, I hurt my back and saw my first and only stint on the disabled list. While out of action, Bill was brought to the Major Leagues and hit around nine home runs in the three weeks I was out. The handwriting was on the wall for me; I was sure to be on the bench for the rest of the season. But one day before my return from the disabled list, Bill got hurt and was out the rest of the year. With that, I returned to the field!

I knew that I would not be the Brewers' catcher for 1985, so I asked for a trade from the Brewers. In so doing, I leveraged myself from being traded to any of the MLB teams to a much smaller list. Texas was not on the list, though they put up a plea for me to return. Kansas City was on the list.

Since I had asked for the trade, my significant trade bonus was now off the table. This is where it gets really cool. On Monday before my trade to Kansas City, a sports writer who I once knew in Texas was now covering another team. He called me and asked if I had heard anything about being traded to Kansas City. Dick Howser, the Royals manager, had made a statement that "if the Royals could get Sundberg" (not *Sandberg*) with my leadership and their great young staff, then "the KC club could win the World Series." The great thing about baseball is that if someone doesn't like you, somebody else probably does.

I told the sports writer that Kansas City was one of the teams on the list given to Milwaukee, but I had heard nothing else. Before hanging up the phone, I asked him if he would let me know about anything he heard.

On Thursday afternoon, the writer called me back and said he heard the deal was done and would be announced on Friday. I immediately picked up the phone and called the MLB offices and withdrew my trade demand, which put my bonus money back on the table. Maybe you see where this is going ...

On Friday morning, Harry Dalton called me stuttering around and then said, "We have a deal with the KC Royals, but we see you withdrew your trade demand, and we want to know about the money in the trade clause."

I answered and said, "I'll meet you halfway."

He replied, "You got it!" So, I got another trade bonus and was off to Kansas City and an '85 World Championship!

The year of public abuse helped me grow and understand how God is at work, even in difficult situations. It took a couple of years to see it all unfold, but those obstacles turned into opportunities.

You may encounter many defeats, but you must not be defeated.

MAYA ANGELOU

Day 41 Meditation

PROMISE

> So, what does all this mean? If God has determined to stand with us, tell me, who then could ever stand against us?
>
> ROMANS 8:31, TPT

MUSIC

Listen to ***Holy Water*** by We The Kingdom.

REFLECTION

- Do you believe that when a window closes to one opportunity that God will open another? Why or why not?

  _____
  _____
  _____
  _____
  _____
  _____

- When was a time when you can look back and see God was at work during a trial?

  _____
  _____
  _____
  _____
  _____
  _____

JOURNAL A PRAYER

_____
_____
_____
_____
_____
_____
_____
_____

WHAT IS THE FATHER SAYING TO YOU?

_____
_____
_____
_____
_____
_____
_____
_____

Day 42
WRESTLE AND WAIT

The third incident happened just a few years ago while I was serving as Sr. Executive Vice President with the Texas Rangers. Nolan Ryan, the President, and I fought a good fight to bring a successful team and a family-friendly, fan-friendly atmosphere to the organization. At one time toward the end, we looked up and agreed that while we had accomplished most of what we set out to do with fans and employees, the environment, and two trips to the World Series in five years, we had only experienced about six months of peace.

Nolan left the club after the '13 season, and I stayed until mid-season of 2014. Though I had intentions to stay in baseball until I turned 70, things between the club and me grew sour, and I decided to part ways with them.

In the last four years, since I left baseball, I have experienced my best years spiritually and in my personal life. This book is a reflection of the time away to reflect. Even that last obstacle has now turned into an opportunity. But for this to happen, I had to be willing to wrestle, wait, and deal with discomfort. Easy does not always equal better.

A little more persistence, a little more effort, and what seemed hopeless may turn to glorious success.

ELBERT HUBBARD

Day 42 Meditation

PROMISE

> Blessed is the man who remains steadfast under trial, for when he has stood the test, he will receive the crown of life, which God has promised to those who love him.
>
> Let no one say when he is tempted, "I am being tempted by God," for God cannot be tempted with evil, and he himself tempts no one. But each person is tempted when he is lured and enticed by his own desire.
>
> JAMES 1:12-16, ESV

MUSIC

Listen to ***Sleep in the Storm*** by Unspoken.

REFLECTION

- Waiting on the Lord is not easy! What happened the last time you had to wait patiently on Him?

_____

_____

_____

_____

_____

_____

JOURNAL A PRAYER

WHAT IS THE FATHER SAYING TO YOU?

Day 43
UNDYING COMMITMENT

In my battle to find emotional, and therefore, spiritual freedom, I've made some observations about the journey. The struggle to break free from the emotional cords restricting freedom is a mega battle, and not a trip most will enter willingly. At times, the journey to emotional freedom feels like your heart is being ripped out of your chest. Yet any struggle for newness of heart is evidenced by this tangible experience. In reality, the Father is healing the hurts and reshaping the heart's new nature into one that can better love Him and others.

The deeper the wounds, the more elements have to be confronted to wipe out the darkness. It holds on like a rabid animal flailing before its death. It is not a pretty picture to observe either in nature or internally while the heart takes a new shape.

Elements that offer an opportunity for empowerment are things like time, wise counsel, loving support, faithful prayer, God's presence, and the sufferer's undying commitment to freedom. These are all weapons needed to overcome and conquer. This is the most courageous journey of all!

The enemy of your soul is out of control. Evil torments. Evil causes havoc and chaos and unrest in all directions. Evil drives you, condemns you, pushes you to the edge, and makes you feel unworthy and unloved.

Love, however, is the extreme opposite. Love is full of grace and truth and does not force its way on you. Love respects others and is patient—it waits for its turn to speak truth when the time is right for you to hear and respond.

The journey of freedom comes in waves like a windy day at the seashore. One wave hits hard, and then there is a break before the next wave hits. At some point, the wind subsides, and a day of calm comes.

I have had four significant periods of counseling where once some freedom was experienced; there was an intentional move toward the tangible feelings of good. I wanted to stay there for a while. All the while, however, I knew there was more work to do. It's a natural process toward the heart's cry for a cure. It is as if deep calls out to deep saying, "I need an emotional break, I need some rest before I can be spoken to about the next piece of my healing."

Thankfully, there is an ebb and flow towards freedom as the heart is reshaped for its real purpose in life and preparation for eternity. There is no experience like it—not even hitting a home run in front of thousands of cheering fans can compare!

Our wounds are often the openings into the best and most beautiful parts of us.

DAVID RICHO

Day 43 Meditation

PROMISE

> All things have been handed over to me by my Father, and no one knows the Son except the Father, and no one knows the Father except the Son and anyone to whom the Son chooses to reveal Him.
>
> MATH 11:27, ESV
>
> Father, You have entrusted me with all that You are and all that You have. No one fully knows the Son except the Father. And no one fully knows the Father except the Son. But the Son is able to introduce and reveal the Father to anyone he chooses.
>
> LUKE 10:22, TPT

MUSIC

Listen to **Nothing Else** by Cody Carnes.

REFLECTION

- What is the cry of your heart? What will cause you to say, "nothing else will do"?

_____

_____

_____

_____

JOURNAL A PRAYER

WHAT IS THE FATHER SAYING TO YOU?

WHAT MATTERS MOST

Time after time, God has shown me that He is working even the most frustrating and difficult circumstances for my good. I have learned to view obstacles as opportunities to develop greater character, gain insight, hone my skills, and step into blessings.

As you think back on hard circumstances and recognize the hand of God guiding you through them, what matters most to you?

Chapter Ten

MASTERFUL MENTOR

As iron sharpens iron,
so one person sharpens another.

—PROVERBS 27:17, NIV

… LEGACY PLAYBOOK

Day 44
LISTEN WELL

It has not been easy to find good mentors, either professionally or spiritually. Mentors are hard to come by, but if you are fortunate enough to find one, listen well, and hold onto them for as long as you can.

I spent only one year in the minors; I made it to the big leagues on my defense skills, so hitting would have to be learned on the job. The first three half and a half years were tough, but once the right mentor was found, my hitting game really improved and went well for several years.

When you are struggling, everyone wants to provide you with "how-to" instructions. Everybody has a theory and an idea to help you, but finding the right person to listen to is vital. My dad had always told me to keep my elbows up. Others talked about stance, weight shift, the angle of the bat on my load, and so forth.

One day, I headed out the front door to retrieve the morning paper when the ten-year-old newspaper boy saw me. When he recognized who I was, he turned his bike around to come back and tell me what he thought I could do to hit better. I tried to run back into the house, but he was faster. What a humbling moment that was! Clearly, I needed help, so it was essential to find the best person to advise me, and then give my ear to them.

In 1975 I hit a disappointing .199434673217. As many ways as you can possibly try to run the numbers to turn the average into .200, the effort didn't work. Whichever way you looked at my average, it was still .199. I had to stare at the .199 number on every baseball card made my entire career—how embarrassing!

The game load managers were asking me to catch did not help. I never once said I was tired even though my September performances were revealing. I finished my first year in 1974, catching 132 games. Then I committed to play winter ball in Venezuela for parts of October and November of that same year. I put another 40 games on my body down south of the border before coming back in 1975 to add 155 games—still an American League record. I was dragging myself to the ballpark by the end of '75, having caught 327 games in eighteen months.

The problem I had with hitting was pulling the ball into the ground to the left side of the infield for outs. This caused my average to dip below my first-year average of .250. The late Jim Fergosi, a teammate in 1976, began to work with me on hitting the ball to right field by using my hands to "inside out the ball." This is a term used to teach good-hitting fundamentals, demonstrating how hands moved through the strike zone to hit the ball.

I trained hard and listened well for an entire year to try to hit the ball to right field during batting practice without ever accomplishing the skill in a game. One entire year! The frustration, anxiety, and disappointment were enormous to experience. A player in the major leagues has about four years on the front end of a career to figure stuff out, even with the high standing of a major prospect, and I was running out of time. It was in my fourth year, mid-way through the 1977 season, when it finally clicked in a game. I still remember the day, June 28, 1977.

Even the Rangers back up catcher came to me in June and said, "Jim, if you don't start hitting, I'll have your job!" The owner of the Texas Rangers, Brad Corbett, also came to me in June and asked if there was anything he could do to help. I heard what he was saying. I could tell by the tone of his words used that my time was running short.

Mentors often help us make corrections in our lives as they breathe a word of encouragement or caution. My best mentor ever came when I accepted Jesus just before July of '77. Everything came together for me professionally for several years following this.

The front cover of the July 28, 1978 issue of The Sporting News had a picture of me titled, "Best Backstop?" In the one year from June 1977 to July 1978, I hit over .330, winning another Gold Glove, which led the newspaper to suggest that I might be the best catcher at that time.

The journey was challenging. I experienced lots of failure and many days of frustration, but with a good mentor, listening well, using the right practice fundamentals, and my willingness to keep pressing on and picking myself up after defeat, paved the way.

Learning to know God and how He interacts with you is no different. He is the best mentor you will ever have.

One of the greatest values of mentors is the ability to see ahead what others cannot see and to help them navigate a course to their destination.

JOHN C. MAXWELL

Day 44 Meditation

PROMISE

> If someone believes they have a relationship with God but fails to guard his words, then his heart is drifting away, and his religion is shallow and empty.
>
> JAMES 1:26, TPT

MUSIC

Listen to ***Not in a Hurry*** by Will Reagan and United Pursuit.

REFLECTION

- Do you talk more than you listen? What will make you want to listen more?

_____

_____

_____

_____

_____

_____

_____

JOURNAL A PRAYER

WHAT IS THE FATHER SAYING TO YOU?

Day 45
THE GIFT

Baseball also provided a platform for me to deal with my ADHD. Our daughter, Briana, was diagnosed with ADD while in the third grade. After listening to the doctor concerning her condition, I could easily trace this back to me, then to my dad, and then to his mother. Who knows how far back it goes beyond there?

One day the doctor said to me, "Jim, did you know that about 75% of all the young boys I see are catchers?" Apparently, catching is a natural for the condition. It is a gift. Whenever I detect a boy with ADD, I now tell all mothers that little piece of brilliance!

Catching gave me a way to work out my lack of focus, release all my energy, and let it loose out on the field. My antennas were moving in every direction to see all the stuff going on. My ADHD equipped me to move teammates based on pitch selection, see things in advance, direct traffic on the field, hear important commands from the manager, and eventually block out the crowd. It was nothing to fear; it was something just to do!

It's an amazing miracle to imagine how a loving God would teach a person with ADHD and listening problems how to listen. Ultimately, my ADHD was a gift, not a handicap. It took grit to see it as such eventually. I would often find myself sitting at an early dinner with my family before an evening game, unaware of their presence. Sometimes Janet would jolt me back from my next game with, "Jim, where are you? We want you to be present here with us!"

While growing up, it was easy to hide in my head. I learned to go there and avoid others because of the full-court press on baseball, which was talked about all the time. So, here I was again in my head with my own family, disrespecting our time together. Also, from my baseball training over the years, I had learned to block out the noise around me. While standing in the batter's box with forty thousand people yelling, I did not hear them. It's convicting to think I considered my family to be noise and interrupting my thoughts.

What's even more amazing is that as I got better at listening to the Spirit, I got better at sitting and listening to others. There seemed to be a connection between the desire to listen and show love to the Most High by showing others love by paying attention to what they had to say. It's even more remarkable for me to be in this place to help encourage you on this pathway. The Holy Spirit is a change agent. Something has shifted, both in my heart and in my brain chemistry, for this to happen.

Day 45 Meditation

PROMISE

> But when the Father sends the Spirit of Holiness, the One like me who sets you free, He will teach you all things in My name. And He will inspire you to remember every word that I've told you.
>
> JOHN 14:26, TPT

MUSIC

Listen to *You Say* by Lauren Daigle.

"What others may see as a disability, I see as a challenge. This challenge is a gift because I have to become stronger to get around it, and smarter to figure out how to use it; others should be so lucky."

— SHANE E. BRYAN

REFLECTION

- What in your life have you seen as a handicap that might actually be a gift from God?

  _____
  _____
  _____

- How can you reframe this in your mind?

  _____
  _____
  _____

JOURNAL A PRAYER

WHAT IS THE FATHER SAYING TO YOU?

WHAT MATTERS MOST

Receiving the benefit of wise counsel has taught me a great deal. I know the value of being mentored not only by a person, but also by the Counselor—the Holy Spirit. Becoming a mentor to others has been one of the greatest privileges I've ever known. Mentoring allows me the opportunity to pass on legacy!

Reflect on those who have mentored you and think about what they have taught you. Now, with a view to creating and passing on your own legacy, what matters most to you?

_____

_____

_____

_____

_____

_____

_____

_____

_____

_____

_____

Chapter Eleven

ADVANCING PRESENCE

"Behold, I am with you and will keep you wherever you go ..."
—GENESIS 28:15, ESV

LEGACY PLAYBOOK

Day 46
RHYTHM OF TRAINING

To be a good major league player, I had to learn practice effectiveness. This was drilled into me from my childhood. I can still hear my dad saying, "Jim, if you want to be really good at anything, you need to practice."

Practicing baseball was easy—a delight. Since the practice field was so convenient from our house, it was not hard to put myself in the appropriate location to practice successfully. While I'm not necessarily a formula person when it comes to experiencing God and walking in faith, there are disciplines in life for which a formula for the principles of practice work.

PASSION + REGULARITY + RIGHT FUNDAMENTALS
+ PERSEVERANCE OVER TIME = SUCCESS

Baseball was my passion, and practice was a daily activity throughout the entire summer. I used a good set of foundational principals for hitting, fielding, and throwing. As a boy, I could run like a deer, but as my career played out, the prolonged periods of squatting eventually got the best of me. Late in my career, whenever I ran, it looked like I was carrying a piano on my back!

If you take four players with equal ability, how does one become better than the others? If their abilities are the same, and the frequency of practice is identical, what wins the day? Well, my answer has to be passion and perseverance. These two ingredients, combined with knowing how to best position oneself to activate practice, will give a player an advantage.

So, how long does it take to practice and become good at something? A better question may be, how important is it to you to make something a priority? In other words, how passionate about it are you?

It took many years of dedicated practice at amateur ball to position myself to succeed at a professional level. But once I was in a position to succeed at the major league level, it took only a short time to tweak my game to its best performance level.

Becoming a good major league ball player and learning how to hear God have one major thing in common. Perseverance. No matter the discouragement, you must keep picking yourself up after defeat and charge forward. A baby first connects hearing and understanding words before they learn to speak. They utter a lot of gibberish and are sometimes frustrated as they learn to communicate. Eventually, gibberish becomes syllables, syllables become words, words become sentences, and they learn to express themselves in ways others can understand.

Practice.

Seeking to hear and see God at work around you requires passion and perseverance. It takes practice. Only by seeking Him first—wanting to hear Him and willing to obey—can you begin to find Him regularly. The more you get to know Him and His word, the greater your effectiveness will be. I encourage you to practice sitting in a place of quiet and rest with a journal to write what you want to say to Him and what He says back to you. God wants to talk with you and desires an active, intimate relationship. It takes time. Practice. The fruitfulness is better than you can possibly imagine.

ADVANCING PRESENCE

Day 46 Meditation

PROMISE

> Isn't it obvious that all runners on the racetrack keep on running to win, but only one receives the victor's prize? Yet each one of you must run the race to be victorious.
>
> A true athlete will be disciplined in every respect, practicing constant self-control in order to win a laurel wreath that quickly withers. But we run our race to win a victor's crown that will last forever.
>
> 1 CORINTHIANS 9:23-25, TPT

MUSIC

Listen to **Raise a Hallelujah** by Jonathan David Helser.

REFLECTION

- At what level is your passion for hearing God's voice and knowing His counsel? Are you willing to employ the fundamentals of practice to your relationship with God?

_____

- What would that look like for you?

_____

_____

_____

_____

JOURNAL A PRAYER

WHAT IS THE FATHER SAYING TO YOU?

Day 47
SOMETHING WONDERFUL

One of the most dramatic times I heard from God was in the early years of my faith during the '85 playoffs between the Toronto Blue Jays and the Kansas City Royals. The Royals were not favored to win against Toronto because on paper; the Blue Jays had the better team.

We had just concluded a game played in Kansas City where we beat the Blue Jays to win game five of the series. This decreased Toronto's lead from two games to one. Prior to this series, no team in MLB history had ever come from a three-game to one deficit to win a playoff series. The win felt good, and now we had to fly back to Toronto for a tough final two games in an attempt to win the American League Championship and a trip to the World Series.

After the game, the team was on a charter flight to Canada, and there was a beautiful sunset that I observed from my window seat. The booming thunderheads and lightning flashed their extraordinary brilliance at a distance, and I marveled at how God had delivered me from the fear of flying. It was now something delightful. I once sat in an aisle seat paralyzed, unable to look out a window. Now, I not only loved and requested a window seat, but sometimes I fell asleep with my face pressing against the window.

Since we were on a charter, each player and their wives had a full row—no one got stuck in the middle seat! Janet and I had a seat between us, and as I talked with her, I would look intermittently out the window. As I took in the view, I heard in my spirit, "Something wonderful is going to happen!" I was elated. The voice was so clear. My anticipation grew.

It amazes me how God used an environment I once feared to speak to me on this magnitude. With a tear in my eye, not something you allow in front of teammates, I slid down into my chair a little deeper.

What was this all about? The thought came to me that I had never before been vulnerable enough to have a group of people pray for me. I had done this before this series out of fear of making a bad mistake. Most players in my era made comments like, "If you make a mistake, you don't want to do it in a post season game where everyone will remember it." Do you remember Billy Buckner in the '86 World Series between Boston and the New York Mets? A ball went right between his legs! It was just a few years ago when the Red Sox won the World Series that one of the headlines in the paper read, "Boston now forgives Buckner."

As I sat pondering a moment unlike anything before experienced, Janet said to me, "What's going on?" I tried to communicate the moment with her as she listened lovingly. We sat there for a few minutes, pondering the possibilities of the message.

Game six came and went as the Royals now evened the series to three wins each. This would push the play offs to a final game seven. What I had experienced on the plane prior to Toronto did not seem confirmed during game six. Did the message mean we would win the series, or was it something else? I wondered.

The atmosphere for game seven in Toronto was as electric as one can imagine. Innings passed, and by the sixth frame, we had a one-run lead with Steve Balboni coming to hit with runners at first and second base. I moved into the on-deck circle without realizing this would be the moment the Messenger on the plane had talked about.

I prepared myself to hit off Dave Stieb. With the deafening noise from the crowd, I went through a hitter's check-list—what was Steib likely to throw me? In the past, he started me off with a slider. Get a good pitch, Jim, make him throw a good strike.

While in the on-deck circle, I heard in my spirit, "This is the moment." The words were penetrating as I paused and looked behind me to see if someone had said something. No one was there! I turned back to focus on the coming plate appearance. A couple of pitches went by, and then I heard, "Get ready, the bases will be loaded." *What is going on? This is like no other experience I've had?* Sure enough, a couple of pitches later, Steve walked to load the bases.

I can't tell you what I thought from the on-deck circle to the batter's box. It was a strange walk of focus. There was a sense of destiny in play—a time planned long before my birth that mirrored participation from God through the gifts He had given me. I do remember stepping into the batter's box thinking Dave Stieb would start me off with a slider, and sure enough, the first pitch slider was too low for ball one. I really wanted to hit the slider, but it would go against my training, which dictated I get a good first pitch to hit.

Then the strangest thing happened during the next pitch. As I again looked and thought slider, Dave Stieb threw me a fastball. Against every fundamental of my training, I couldn't stop my hands from exploding toward the ball with bat in hand. Hitters are trained to only swing at pitches they are looking for until two strikes. I was looking for a slider and swung at a fastball. It was an out of body experience that is hard to explain. It's almost like something else took over.

The swing caused me to loft the ball high down the right-field line with a wind blowing toward the corner foul pole. As I exited the batter's box, it felt like something was holding my body back. It was hard to run, like a dream where I had trouble moving my feet as I ran from a giant chasing me. My feet seemed to stick to the ground in slow motion as I followed the ball with my eyes.

Jesse Barfield looked to be tracking the ball as he ran back toward the fence and then leaped to catch the ball. The centerfield camera angle would later show that Jesse's tall, husky frame would strike the fence at the same time as the ball hit the top of the fence.

When I saw the ball hit on top of the fence, I thought, *Is it going over the fence, or will it stay in play with the need to run?* As the ball hit on top, it glanced into play, and the slow-motion concluded its turtle-like advance back to normal time. All the runners crossed the plate in front of me, and I stood at third base with a triple! It was the most amazing experience I ever had on the field! Standing at third base while watching my teammates go crazy, I wanted to leave the base to join them, but it would have to wait.

The rest is history. We were off to the World Series! In that moment, all the previous struggles and difficulties of the past dissipated into thanksgiving. God wants a relationship with us, and He takes pleasure in our victories as we cooperate with the way He has created us.

Day 47 Meditation

PROMISE

Right at the crest, where Mount Olives begins its descent, the whole crowd of disciples burst into enthusiastic praise over all the mighty works they had witnessed:

Blessed is He who comes, the king in God's name!
All's well in heaven!
Glory in the high places!

LUKE 19:37-38, MSG

ADVANCING PRESENCE

*What we are is God's gift to us.
What we become is our gift to God.*

ELEANOR POWELL

MUSIC

Listen to **Revelation Song** by Kari Jobe.

REFLECTION

- What is it that God has aligned with you to do?

  _____
  _____
  _____
  _____

- How does this make you feel?

  _____
  _____
  _____

JOURNAL A PRAYER

_____

_____

_____

_____

_____

_____

_____

_____

WHAT IS THE FATHER SAYING TO YOU?

_____

_____

_____

_____

_____

_____

_____

_____

Day 48
THE DISCIPLINE OF PRACTICE

One of the best things that ever happened to me was leaving the workplace before I had intended. I planned to work until I turned seventy; instead, my departure occurred at sixty-three. As mentioned before, the Texas Rangers and I parted ways in mid-2014 after a very successful run in which the Rangers made two trips to the World Series in 2010 and 2011. I had no idea that after thirty-five years in baseball, what the next four years would encompass.

I spent the next couple of years somewhat on my face in rest, recouping from the last eight difficult months. All the while, I was asking God to speak. At first, I could not hear Him because I used to moving into the next thing to do. After a while, I eventually got the message to put "doing" on hold and learn how to "be" with Him. This was not easy to do after always being active in the pursuit of a purpose. I was used to being driven by the next goal. I had always been proactive about the next phase, whatever that might look like. It wasn't until five months after finding out I had cancer that I submitted fully to the request to "be" and rest.

I left for Loma Linda, California, for cancer treatment. They were the first place to use Proton therapy for prostate cancer. It took me seven weeks after starting therapy before I surrendered. I had taken a lot of material with me to study and work on. Finally, I scrapped it all, threw up my hands, and said, "Okay, teach me to 'be' in Your presence. I'll submit my 'doing' to flow out of my 'being' with You!" It changed my life—I wish I had done it earlier!

During my ten weeks of treatment, we learned to love the west coast and those who live there in the southern California area. How can you not with the mountains and their beautiful beaches? This was not necessarily the way I got to experience places during my baseball days. Throughout my career, most of what I saw in the LA area was limited to flying in and out at night, riding buses at night to and from LAX until John Wayne airport opened. Then I rode on buses to Anaheim stadium with smog so thick I couldn't even see the mountain ranges even though they were really close. Generally, I was confined to my hotel room to rest before the next game. But while getting treatment, Janet and I traveled everywhere in the area. We made it an extended vacation instead of dwelling on cancer treatment, which was amazingly easy and painless as compared to most other types of treatment.

A few months after returning home, I was led into really discovering what "being" in God's presence was all about. At a Quest Life event, I learned to ask God to give me "eyes to see and ears to hear." I decided to commit to pursuing God daily by requesting a greater sense of His presence in my life. The intent was to make it a habit, so I decided to get all I could and shoot for fifty days of exploring God in which I journaled the amazing journey. It started in the morning during my time alone, and soon I began to carry it further into the day. I stumbled a few times as one does when they begin to walk in a new way, but after a period, I began to realize that God was driving the activity with the things I heard and saw from Him.

This may not seem like a big deal, but it was to me, and it was to Him. One morning, I was taking the dry cleaning in and drove across railroad tracks, as I have done numerous times. Anyone who knows me knows I love trains. Actually, a few of my grandchildren also love them and share in watching them with me. As I drove over the tracks and looked right, there was a long straightaway with a bend almost a mile away. I've never seen a train come around the bend, and I asked God to allow me to see that sometime. When I dropped the clothes off and headed back across the tracks, now looking to my left, there came a train around the bend.

What hit me is that it was His prompting, which caused me to request something from Him that He knew was just about to happen. He drove the request and then answered it. Wow!

I'm now seeing things I've never seen and hearing things I've never heard before and loving it. I see and hear Him even in what might seem minimal, but that's who He is and how He loves. But you first have to be aware to look and listen, or you will miss it.

As I was approaching the end of my fifty days of "eyes to see and ears to hear," there was the urge to take it longer. So, I determined to go for one hundred days because of the encouragement and what it was doing to my heart. Later, I expanded it to one hundred and fifty-three days because of a number I saw while reading scripture one day. The amount of days is not important, but I know from all my years of training that practice makes permanent, so I pressed forward. I'll save what happened in the last week of the one hundred fifty-three days for my next entry.

In the progress of God's redemptive work, communication advances into communion, and communion into union.

DALLAS WILLARD

Day 48 Meditation

PROMISE

Ears to hear and eyes to see—both are gifts from the Lord.

PROVERBS 20:12, NLT

MUSIC

Listen to **Defender** by Rita Springer.

REFLECTION

- The discipline of practice anticipates a return on investment. What is your prize?

  _____
  _____
  _____

- What disciplined practice have you put into place?

  _____
  _____
  _____
  _____

JOURNAL A PRAYER

WHAT IS THE FATHER SAYING TO YOU?

Day 49
TAKING RISKS

We headed to Colorado, trailering our Harley Motorcycle with a couple of weeks left in my one hundred fifty-three days of "eyes to see and ears to hear." The discipline had long since settled in to be natural. It was no longer something to practice but a natural flow. Colorado is a great place to drive in the summer, but biking it is grand!

Janet and I left one morning to go to Steamboat Springs for lunch. We had made this trip before and returned to Vail. It was a nice day trip of about 235 miles with the routes we took. Prior to lunch, as we drove into Steamboat Springs, I was picking up on something dark or heavy in my spirit. Clouds were building, and I was trying to discern if the Spirit was trying to give me a heads up about the weather or something else. This wasn't the first time I had gotten pre-warning about something like this. We had a great time doing one of our favorite things. Having a date with a pleasant dining experience was great, but the heaviness didn't pass. I hadn't told Janet how I was feeling at this point.

We left the restaurant, climbed on the bike with our rain gear, and headed south out of town. We were coming to a crossroads where we could go one of two directions while waving goodbye to a couple we got to know during lunch. They went the direction we came from, but I decided to take a different route back up over the mountain that overlooked the valley with a gorgeous view.

Toward the top of our climb, my Spirit grew more concerned, "Is it the weather, Lord? Are you telling me to turn around or take cover?" I listened, but I really didn't hear anything. At that point, I noticed a man in a truck behind us a couple of hundred feet back was driving erratically.

The driver would speed up slightly, then slow down and weave into the other part of a two-lane road as we moved across the flat part of the mountain top area.

A couple of things were running through my mind. *1) Has he been drinking or on some drug? 2) Should I pull over and let him pass?* All of a sudden, he sped up so fast I thought he was going to hit us. Then he stopped. He was so close that Janet heard the sound of his engine over the sound of the Harley. He backed off again and continued to drive unpredictably. With one eye glued to my rearview mirror, the other was looking for a place to move over and stop.

We reached an area for a turn, and by now, we knew the driver was a male, looking to turn and leave our road. All of a sudden, he continued forward in the wrong lane before coming in back behind us. At this point, I couldn't exit the road because of a steep drop off to my right with a mountain tracking the other side. As we were approaching a turn to the left, and with no vision to oncoming traffic, he randomly moved again, just missing my back bumper. Then he sped away in the wrong lane at high velocity before moving back into our lane and exiting around the corner out of sight.

I was both thankful and concerned when I clearly heard, "Stop for the accident!" Before I could even think or process what I thought I heard, we came around the corner to see the man in the truck make an impact with an enormous asphalt roller machine parked along the side the road. He collided with it at high speed, and there was a small explosion without fire.

It happened in a split second. As the pickup truck veered across the lane, two oncoming motorcycle drivers swerved into our lane to avoid contact. We all stopped our bikes, and the other drivers looked to be in shock as the truck had barely missed them.

We all turned our bikes off and went to the aid of the driver. He hit the parked machine so hard that it threw everything in the back of his truck fifty to one hundred feet forward onto the slightly declining mountain. It's not easy to witness an accident, let alone be the first responders approaching the vehicle to check out the condition of the driver. The driver of the truck was unconscious and the engine block in the front seat where a passenger would have sat.

I approached the driver, first asking God, "What is this about, and what do you want me to do?" I believe I heard God say, "It's too late for him but turn around." When I turned around, the other two motorcycle guys were standing there. The three of us tried to talk to the driver while Janet called authorities. The man never gained consciousness and died while we were there shortly after medics, and the state trooper arrived. No one could pry the door open, not even the back door.

In the time the other two drivers and I were together, I learned a little bit about them and, with a nudge, asked them where they stood in their relationship with God because He had just spared them from death. It's obvious the experience had moved us all, and within three hours we were on our way.

During the next couple of days, I wrestled with trying to put all the pieces together with only some sense of clarity. Janet couldn't find out a drug or alcohol report, but through her research found out there was another traffic fatality the same day on the same road in a slightly different location and time.

What does one do with that? I was never taught in church how to have a conversation with God. Many people don't believe it's possible to converse with the Spirit, while others seem to think that when God speaks, He quotes scripture. But there is a spirit of the law that is cooperative with the letter of the law. In other words, whatever you hear will be consistent with scripture and aligned with God's character.

For days, I revisited the words I knew I heard; some were deep in my spirit, others seeming to be words heard. I wrestled with how to make some sense of it all, but one thing was clear. Because of my quest to know Him, hear Him, and see Him at work around me, I believe God was letting me in on a major battle in the spiritual realm of which Janet and I were a target. But God said, "NO, NOT TODAY, I STILL HAVE A PLAN FOR YOU!" I do not know the story of the truck driver, why he was on that road that day at that time, but I do know Janet and I were there at His prompting. He had purpose in our positioning that day.

God actually does want to show His beloved how often He protects them, but you have to be listening and looking to become aware. We saw God's protection that day in a different way, and it changed us from that point forward. He makes me brave. He gives me courage to press forward against adversity. We can't be afraid of moving into danger, or we risk not seeing God's powerful presence at work. Trust in the Lord, and be courageous!

• • •

Let every man abide in the calling wherein he is called and his work will be as sacred as the work of the ministry. It is not what a man does that determines whether his work is sacred or secular, it is why he does it.

A.W. TOZER

Day 49 Meditation

PROMISE

> The Lord will keep you from all harm—He will watch over your life; the Lord will watch over your coming and going both now and forevermore.
>
> PSALM 121:7-8, NIV

> But You, Lord, are a shield around me, my glory, the One who lifts my head high. I call out to the Lord, and He answers me from His holy mountain. I lie down and sleep; I wake again because the Lord sustains me.
>
> PSALM 3:3-5, NIV

MUSIC

Listen to ***Take Me to the King*** by Tamela Mann.

REFLECTION

- How well do you hear God's voice? How has your relationship with God caused you to step into danger or move you to take a risk?

_____

_____

_____

_____

JOURNAL A PRAYER

WHAT IS THE FATHER SAYING TO YOU?

Day 50
I GOT THIS!

In August of 2016, I was told, "Jim, you have cancer." Those of you who have heard those words spoken to you know the shock. Emotions begin to rise from deep places previously unknown to you. Your mind races. Fear envelopes. The world stops spinning for a moment.

Before that fateful visit, I had my routine annual exam. A few days later, my doctor called and said, "If these levels don't go down in a couple of months, then we need to take another step."

"Okay," I answered. He didn't sound too threatening, I had been there before and learned not to be alarmed.

In a follow-up exam several months later, the levels in my blood had not reduced, so I was sent to a specialist. The specialist prescribed antibiotics as part of the protocol and waited two more weeks before ordering new blood work. That test showed only a slight improvement in numbers. I suggested to the doctor that we try antibiotics one more time but increase the strength and wait three weeks to recheck. The doctor said he had something better in mind.

A new MRI procedure designed to check specific cells in a targeted area had just been introduced. So, the plan was to have this new MRI procedure. The test was not intended to detect cancer cells, but rather to locate any suspicious cells and give them a rating of one to five. A four or five rating would indicate the need for a biopsy of that tissue.

I went for the MRI and returned to the specialist a few weeks later to hear the results. I decided to put my learning into play and invited the

Lord to help by asking, "What is going on here?" Right before entering the doctor's office, I clearly heard, "Jim, there is something there, but I got it!"

WOW! Okay! A supernatural calm came over me as I walked through the door. In moments, the doctor walked in and didn't waste any time. "Jim," he said, "some of the cells show up as a four and five from the MRI, so we need to set up a biopsy." He went on to assure me that it was just precautionary and that the procedure would clarify any issues. "In fact," he said, "this new MRI will give the physician performing the biopsy targets to highlight while hitting other areas as a precaution."

"Alright," I answered, but I knew something more was going on.

I was in Galesburg, visiting my dad and having lunch when the doctor called. "Jim, you have cancer, and a few of the cells are very aggressive." My heart started to pound as I grasped for something emotionally to hold on to. "Who's on the phone, son," my dad asked. I waved him off, not wanting to say anything then. Why add to the potential panic? I stared down at my plate, unsure of where to direct the conversation, and just then, the words came back to me, "There is something there, but I got it!"

The words were an invitation into the supernatural with Him. His presence was there to calm my natural emotions! The prompting to ask for help all those weeks ago was an object lesson in faith. It was His invitation to bring peace into a situation that would typically result in anxiety. I resolved to continue in dialogue with Him to hear comfort in His words in the midst of the doctor's voices ringing with disquieting news. The Spirit's words would keep me secure during the entire time of my cancer treatment and beyond.

God did not fail me in my hour of need, and in the process, I took one more step toward accepting whatever outcome as long as He was with me. As of the writing of this book (May 2020), four years have passed since my diagnosis. I am now cancer free!

My journey to hear His voice and know His presence continues. It is a daily invitation to abide with Him. I still hear Him regularly say, "I got this!" I encourage you to continue asking and listening far beyond our 50 days together. God longs to fellowship with you, and He desires to make Himself known to you in real and tangible ways. Keep going.

Day 50 Meditation

PROMISE

> With my whole heart, with my whole life, and with my innermost being, I bow in wonder and love before You, the holy God!
>
> Yahweh, You are my soul's celebration.
>
> How could I ever forget the miracles of kindness You've done for me?
>
> You kissed my heart with forgiveness, in spite of all I've done.
> You've healed me inside and out from every disease.
> You've rescued me from hell and saved my life.
> You've crowned me with love and mercy.
> You satisfy my every desire with good things.
> You've supercharged my life so that I soar again like a flying eagle in the sky!
>
> PSALM 103:1-5, TPT

MUSIC

Listen to *You're Gonna Be Ok* by Jenn Johnson.

Faith is believing God is going to take you places before you even get there.

MATTHEW BARNETT

REFLECTION

- Have you ever received news that really upended you (job loss, loss of a loved one, difficult diagnosis)? How did you handle it?

- Here at the end of our 50 days together, what have you learned that could help you face hard news with peace?

JOURNAL A PRAYER

WHAT IS THE FATHER SAYING TO YOU?

ADVANCING PRESENCE

WHAT MATTERS MOST

There is an old song that goes, "Every day with Jesus is sweeter than the day before." It's true! The longer I walk with God, the more rich and full and wonderful His presence becomes to me. I am learning to see Him not just in the big life-changing important things but also in the smallest details. His glory and grace never cease to amaze me!

Wherever you are in your walk with the Lord, I invite you to go deeper with Him. When all is said and done and you stand before the throne and weigh things in the balance—your family, your career, your dreams, your friendships, your calling—consider the threads of character which run through all of these areas and write what matters most to you.

The greatest good you can do for another is not just to share your riches but to reveal to him his own.

BENJAMIN DISRAELI

Jim's Mission Statement

WHAT MATTERS MOST TO ME

I have concluded that all the accumulation of wealth, even if I could achieve it, is an insufficient reason for living. Nor is fame of any lasting benefit. When I reach the end of my days, I must be able to look back on more than just Gold Gloves, All-Star Games, World Championships, and records. I will consider my earthly existence to have been wasted unless I recall a loving family, a consistent investment in the lives of people, and an earnest attempt to serve the one and only God, who made me! Nothing else makes much sense.

- LOVING FAMILY
- INVESTMENT IN PEOPLE
- SERVING GOD

Photo Gallery

First Hit, Last Hit, and a Few Milestones in Between

Jim, Janet, and baby Aaron pictured in their Iowa City apartment at the signing of Jim's 1st contract with the Rangers in 1973.

Jim with daughter, Briana, in the TV booth with Steve Busby.

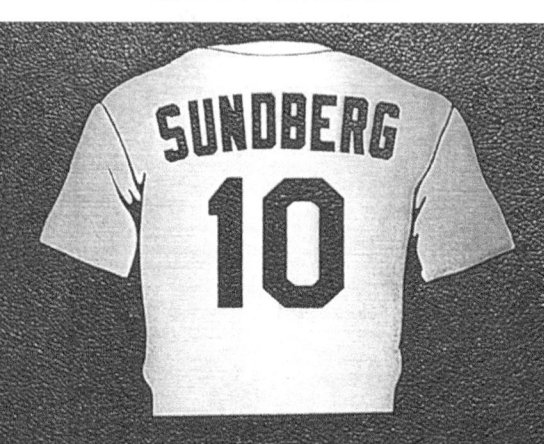

JIM SUNDBERG, C

Playing career: 1974-1989
Years with Rangers: 1974-1983, 1988-1989

A CONSISTENT AND DURABLE PERFORMER BEHIND THE PLATE WHO BECAME FIRST RANGER TO PLAY IN MORE THAN 1,500 GAMES. MADE THE JUMP FROM DOUBLE A TO AMERICAN LEAGUE ALL-STAR IN 1974. CAUGHT 140 OR MORE GAMES FOR SIX STRAIGHT SEASONS FROM 1975-1980. WON SIX CONSECUTIVE GOLD GLOVE AWARDS FROM 1976-1981, SECOND MOST AMONG AL CATCHERS TO IVAN RODRIGUEZ. RANKS AMONG THE CLUBS ALL-TIME LEADERS WITH 1,512 GAMES, 4,684 AT BATS, 482 RUNS, 1,180 HITS, AND 542 WALKS. HAS GIVEN HIS TIME TO COUNTLESS CHARITABLE ENDEAVORS RECOGNIZED BY THE RANGERS' ANNUAL COMMUNITY ACHIEVEMENT AWARD IN HIS NAME. ALSO SAW ACTION WITH THE BREWERS, ROYALS, AND CUBS IN 16 BIG LEAGUE SEASONS.

TEXAS RANGERS
B★A★S★E★B★A★L★L
HALL OF FAME

Inducted August 2, 2003

PHOTO GALLERY

'85 World Series Champions Kansas City Royals on the inside cover of *Sports Illustrated* in the Spring of '86.

Jim with Hall of Fame catchers, Johnny Bench and Iván Rodríguez. This represents 29 Gold Gloves won by the group and signed by all.

LEGACY PLAYBOOK

Jim's childhood dream of playing Major League Baseball came true, and he played for 16 years! Pictured here is his first and last hit along with 4 of 64 baseball cards published.

Son, Aaron, enjoys a little down time on top of the Texas Rangers new spring training dugout in Pompano Beach, Florida (late 70s).

PHOTO GALLERY

Wife, Janet, tries to hit during a family game while Jim interferes!

A determined Janet tries to get her opponent out!

Jim with daughter, Briana, at a 1987 family day with the Cubs in Wrigley Field.

LEGACY PLAYBOOK

Janet with Audra (daughter) and Aaron (son) watching Jim play at Arlington Stadium.

The Sundberg's legacy—their wonderful family gathers for a group photo.

PHOTO GALLERY

Jim reflects on his 16-year MLB career.

Nolan Ryan, Jim Sundberg, and friends with host,
Warren Buffet, in his College World Series suite.

LEGACY PLAYBOOK

The inspirational game-winning slide sequence in Game #6 of the 1985 World Series. Darrell Porter, the Cardinals catcher, got out of position allowing Jim to slide to the back corner of homeplate for a come-from-behind win in the 9th inning.

"And the win, what a thrill!"

"With practical advice, Jim and Janet share how to best parent a child in sports, eliminate the possible frustrations and disappointments, and bring out the best in a sports experience."

DAVE DRAVECKY, PRESIDENT, OUTREACH OF HOPE

"*How to Win at Sports Parenting* puts kids and sports into the proper context for success—personal success and family success."

RICHARD SCHULTZ, EXECUTIVE DIRECTOR UNITED STATES OLYMPIC COMITTEE

SPORTS IS MORE THAN JUST A GAME

Discover how to help your children …

- **Enjoy to the fullest the sports they play**
- **Learn valuable sports-to-life-lessons**
- **Deal with game-day emotions in a healthy manner**
- **Develop crucial skills they will use the rest of their lives**

Drawing from a rich background in sports, parenting, and family development, Jim Sundberg and his wife, Janet, teach that the sports experience can provide unique opportunities for kids to deal with emotions and develop the skills necessary for healthy, life-enhancing, interaction with others. But for this to happen, moms and dads need a practical plan.

The Sundbergs will help you build that plan by showing you *How to Win at Sports Parenting*.

Available at amazon.com and JimSundberg.com

For more information or to book Jim to speak at your conference or event, visit

JimSundberg.com

Made in the USA
Monee, IL
15 January 2024